BRITISH BATTLECRUISER
VS
GERMAN BATTLECRUISER
1914–16

MARK STILLE

First published in Great Britain in 2013 by Osprey Publishing,
PO Box 883, Oxford, OX1 9PL, UK
PO Box 3985, New York, NY 10185-3985, USA
E-mail: info@ospreypublishing.com

Osprey Publishing is part of the Osprey Group

A CIP catalogue record for this book is available from the British Library

Print ISBN: 978 1 78096 096 8
PDF ebook ISBN: 978 1 78096 097 5
ePub ebook ISBN: 978 1 78096 098 2

Index by Sandra Shotter
Typeset in ITC Conduit and Adobe Garamond
Maps by bounford.com
Originated by PDQ Media, Bungay, UK
Printed in China through Asia Pacific Offset Ltd.

13 14 15 16 17   10 9 8 7 6 5 4 3 2 1

Osprey Publishing is supporting the Woodland Trust, the UK's leading
woodland conservation charity, by funding the dedication of trees.

www.ospreypublishing.com

Imperial War Museum Collections

Many of the photos in this book come from the Imperial War Museum's huge
collections which cover all aspects of conflict involving Britain and the
Commonwealth since the start of the twentieth century. These rich resources
are available online to search, browse and buy at www.iwmcollections.org.uk.
In addition to Collections Online, you can visit the Visitor Rooms where you
can explore over 8 million photographs, thousands of hours of moving images,
the largest sound archive of its kind in the world, thousands of diaries and
letters written by people in wartime, and a huge reference library. To make an
appointment, call (020) 7416 5320, or e-mail mail@iwm.org.uk

Imperial War Museum www.iwm.org.uk

Editor's note

All distances quoted are in nautical miles. Weights are given in long tons.

1 nautical mile = 1.85km
1yd = 0.9m
1ft = 0.3m
1in = 2.54cm/25.4mm
1 long ton = 1.016 tonnes
1lb = 0.45kg
1kt = 1.85km/h
1kt = 1.15mph

Artist's note

Readers may care to note that the original paintings from which the cover and
battlescenes of this book were prepared are available for private sale. All
reproduction copyright whatsoever is retained by the Publishers. All enquiries
should be sent via:

www.paulwrightmaritimeartist.co.uk or email p.wright1@btinternet.com

The Publishers regret that they can enter into no correspondence upon this
matter.

CONTENTS

INTRODUCTION

The entire concept of the battlecruiser was the invention of Admiral of the Fleet Sir John 'Jacky' Fisher (1841–1920). As First Sea Lord (the professional head of Britain's Royal Navy) from 1904 to 1911, he instituted a revolution in naval affairs, beginning with the introduction of the all-big-gun battleship. This ship, driven by the recently introduced steam-turbine engines, was faster and more powerful than any other existing battleship. The improvement in capabilities meant that every subsequent ship built to this design was known as a dreadnought, named after the first British ship built to this concept.

Fisher wanted to take his revolution one step further. As powerful as the new dreadnoughts were, Fisher believed they were vulnerable to torpedoes and mines. His preferred ship was the battlecruiser (often seen as 'battle cruiser'), which combined the speed of the armoured cruiser with the all-big-gun armament of the new dreadnought. Since Fisher believed that 'speed is armour', the relatively light scale of protection on the new battlecruiser was not seen as a handicap. These versatile ships would be able to protect British shipping worldwide against commerce raiders as well as serve as a scouting force for the main battle fleet in European waters.

Under conditions of great secrecy, the first British battlecruisers were laid down in 1906 and completed in 1908. The Germans were unaware of the precise characteristics of this new type of ship until the middle of 1906, but quickly moved to match Fisher's newest challenge. By 1907, they had begun construction of their own large cruiser (the Germans did not use the term battlecruiser during the war), and now both sides incorporated construction of battlecruisers into their increasingly expensive and hectic naval construction programmes. From the start, Fisher's invention was controversial. Battlecruisers were extremely expensive to build and did not easily fit into the mould of pre-war doctrine. Armed with dreadnought-type armament, but carrying armour

unable to defend themselves against such weapons, they were incorporated into the battle fleet, and were thus used in a manner that they were not designed for. On both sides of the North Sea, the battlecruiser fleets were seen as the knights of the fleet. Fast and heavily armed, they were always deployed in the vanguard of their respective battle fleets. While the battle fleets spent much of their time in port, the battlecruisers were much more active.

Dreadnought seen shortly after completion. Though her steam turbines gave her a speed of 21 kt – an unheard-of speed for a capital ship – Fisher wanted even higher speed, leading to the advent of the battlecruiser. (NHHC NH 63596)

Naval warfare in the North Sea did not take the course either side expected during the first months of the war. The anticipated great clash of battle fleets did not occur and the Germans struggled to find a way to deal with the distant blockade of Germany mounted by the Royal Navy. Trying to draw portions of the British Fleet into battle where it could be defeated piecemeal, the Germans began a series of raids on towns along Britain's North Sea coast. These were led by the German battlecruisers. One of these resulted in the first clash of battlecruisers on 24 January 1915. In this clash, named the battle of Dogger Bank, five British battlecruisers faced three of their German counterparts (a fourth large German ship was also present, but it was an armoured cruiser). The battle resulted in a British victory since they sank the German armoured cruiser, but it was also a missed opportunity since the outnumbered German battlecruisers escaped. Two of the German battlecruisers were damaged, one heavily. In return, the Germans pounded the British flagship with 17 hits and damaged another battlecruiser. Both sides had reasons to be content since the battlecruisers of both sides seemed to have performed well in their first action.

With a top speed of over 26kt, *Invincible* possessed the ability to outrun any big-gun ship except a German battlecruiser. She was destroyed at Jutland by a magazine explosion. (NHHC NH 60031)

The next battlecruiser action was also the last battlecruiser action of the war. Moreover, it was the only occasion when the two great battle fleets met. This was the battle of Jutland, fought in the eastern North Sea on 31 May 1916 and into the following morning of 1 June. On this occasion, the battlecruisers of both sides were performing their primary function of scouting ahead of the main battle fleets. As usual, the British battlecruiser force was larger with six battlecruisers and four fast battleships. Facing them were all five available German battlecruisers.

The first phase of the action was strictly a battlecruiser duel featuring the six British battlecruisers against their five German counterparts. Unsupported by the attached battleships, the British force suffered badly. Within minutes, the British suffered their first shock when one of their battlecruisers blew up and sank due to a magazine explosion. The disaster was repeated a second time only minutes after the first. The German ships were also taken under heavy fire, and suffered varying degrees of damage, but none were in danger of sinking. The first stage of the action seemed to confirm two key issues – the vulnerability of the battlecruiser in general and the superiority of German designs.

As the action unfolded, the German battlecruisers took increasing damage, but not before they had managed to sink a third British battlecruiser, again when her magazine exploded. As the two fleets were fully engaged in the evening, the German battlecruisers were used to cover the withdrawal of the main German force. Despite the terrific pounding that this entailed, only one German battlecruiser was sunk, and this was due to progressive flooding the next morning as the Germans evaded the British to return to base. The battle was a shock to the Royal Navy. Though it provided a decisive victory in the respect that it maintained the blockade against Germany, the cost had been high. Each of the lost battlecruisers went down with almost their entire crews.

This book examines the concepts behind the battlecruisers of both sides, including their construction and characteristics, and most importantly their use in the two battlecruiser clashes of the war.

After Jutland, *Seydlitz* did not reach the naval base at Wilhelmshaven until 6 June. This photograph clearly shows the extent of the damage to the ship. Repairs took until mid-September, but *Seydlitz* was manifest proof of the toughness of German battlecruisers. (NHHC NH 2407)

CHRONOLOGY

1905
June Fisher's Committee on Designs approves design of first battlecruiser

1906
February *Dreadnought*, the first all-big-gun warship, is launched; *Inflexible*, the first battlecruiser to begin construction, is laid down

August Design work begins on first German battlecruiser

1908
March First German battlecruiser, *Von der Tann*, is laid down

October *Inflexible* and *Indomitable* completed

1909
March *Invincible* completed

1911
February *Von der Tann* is placed in service
April *Indefatigable* completed

1912
March *Moltke* is placed in service
May *Lion* completed
August *Goeben* enters service
November *New Zealand* and *Princess Royal* completed

1913
June *Australia* completed
August *Queen Mary* completed; *Seydlitz* placed in service

Invincible at the battle of the Falkland Islands. This was probably the finest moment for Fisher's pet invention as the two battlecruisers sent to the South Atlantic were employed in the precise role they were built to perform. By the battle of Jutland, these first-generation British battlecruisers were obsolescent. (IWM SP 2092)

1914

4 August	Britain declares war on Germany
10 August	*Goeben* reaches Turkey having escaped the shadowing *Indomitable* and *Indefatigable*
28 August	Battle of the Heligoland Bight: British battlecruisers sink three German light cruisers in the first British naval victory of the war
October	*Tiger* completed
November	*Derfflinger* completed
3 November	German battlecruisers bombard Yarmouth
8 December	Battle of the Falkland Islands: *Invincible* and *Inflexible* destroy two German armoured cruisers
16 December	German battlecruisers bombard Scarborough and escape interception by British battlecruisers

1915

24 January	Battle of Dogger Bank: British battlecruisers sink a German armoured cruiser and damage *Seydlitz* and *Derfflinger*; in exchange *Lion* and *Tiger* are damaged
August	*Lützow* completed, but does not enter service until March 1916

1916

24 April	German battlecruisers bombard Lowestoft
2300hrs, 30 May	British Battlecruiser Fleet departs Rosyth after British learn of impending sortie by German fleet
0100hrs, 31 May	German battlecruisers put to sea
1400hrs, 31 May	German and British ships investigate sighting of a Danish freighter
1428hrs, 31 May	British and German light cruisers exchange fire, opening the battle of Jutland
1548hrs, 31 May	British and German battlecruisers begin to exchange fire
1600hrs, 31 May	Turret on *Lion* penetrated by German shell; magazine flooded to avoid catastrophic explosion
1603hrs, 31 May	*Indefatigable* blows up under fire from *Von der Tann*
1626hrs, 31 May	*Queen Mary* blows up under fire from *Derfflinger* and *Seydlitz*
1834hrs, 31 May	*Invincible* blows up under fire from *Derfflinger*
31 May	*Hood*, the last British battlecruiser, is laid down
0057hrs, 1 June	*Lützow* scuttled after heavy shell damage causes unchecked progressive flooding

1919

June	German battle fleet scuttled at Scapa Flow, including five battlecruisers

DESIGN AND DEVELOPMENT

THE ADVENT OF THE BATTLECRUISER

The originator of the battlecruiser concept was Admiral Fisher. After assuming the post of First Sea Lord on 20 October 1904, he began a programme to modernize the Royal Navy. Among his more radical ideas was the notion that an all-big-gun version of the current armoured cruiser was the warship of the future. Any capital ship design is a trade-off between the competing requirements of firepower, protection and speed. In Fisher's mind, the primary consideration had to be speed since it conferred both tactical and strategic advantages. Secondary in importance was firepower, and protection came in a distant third. This general concept was embodied in the battlecruiser.

The design forerunner of the battlecruiser was the armoured cruiser. These were large ships, usually as long or longer than a contemporary battleship, but less heavily armed and much less armoured. At times, they could be used in the main line of battle, as the Japanese were forced to at the battle of Tsushima in May 1905. As Fisher pushed for his battlecruiser concept, the latest class of British armoured cruiser was HMS *Minotaur*, which carried a mixed main battery of 9.2in and 7.5in guns, possessed a speed of 23kt, and a main armour belt of 6in. This class was designed in 1904, the same time the 'Committee on Designs' was appointed by Fisher to consider the future requirements for warship design. Fisher himself was president of the committee. The

Dreadnought was revolutionary for its all-big-gun design of a main battery of ten 12in guns. When the Royal Navy followed suit and placed an all-big-gun main battery on an armoured cruiser, the result was the battlecruiser. (Library of Congress)

first meeting in January 1905 provided the guidelines for future armoured cruiser construction. It was to have protection on the same scale of *Minotaur*, have a top speed of 25.5kt and carry eight 12in guns. The adoption of the 12in gun was the critical difference. The jump to a 12in gun created a unique new ship that was clearly not just another modified armoured cruiser. It led to the battlecruiser and its subsequent use in the line of battle.

By June 1905, the final design was approved. The 1905–06 programme included the first all-big-gun battleship (the famous *Dreadnought*) and three of the new armoured cruisers. By this time, the displacement of Fisher's new ships had risen to 17,250 tons and the main battery was established at eight 12in guns in four turrets. The four turrets were placed one forward and aft with the other two in waist positions amidships. These amidships turrets were not on the ship's centreline and thus had a very limited arc of fire on their opposite beams. In practice, this meant the class could only employ a six-gun broadside to either beam. Nevertheless, the weight of the 12in shells meant a much greater broadside than the earlier armoured cruisers. The three ships were laid down beginning in February 1906, but the entire group was not finished until 1908.

As was the case on *Dreadnought*, the need for greater speed was addressed by the adoption of steam turbines. For the new battlecruisers, the design speed was 25kt, and

Inflexible was the only British battlecruiser to suffer mine or torpedo damage during the war when she struck a mine on 18 March 1915 during the attack on Turkish forts on the Dardanelles. She survived to re-join the Grand Fleet and fight at Jutland. (Library of Congress)

11

The battlecruiser *Australia* under construction on the Clyde. While the Indefatigable class ships were being built, the Germans were building battlecruisers of the Moltke class, which were a much superior design. (Cody Images)

to achieve this, it was calculated that 31 boilers were needed. This required an increase in length. The ships were fitted with very long forecastles to gain the necessary beam-to-length ratio needed for higher speeds.

The most controversial aspect of the design was the relative lack of armoured protection. In keeping with earlier armoured cruisers, which did not really live up to their name, armoured protection remained on the light side. The first class of improved armoured cruisers was fitted with a main belt with a maximum of 6in of armour. Turrets and barbettes received a maximum of 7in and horizontal protection was patchy, with a maximum of 2.5in. This was an important defect since as the range of guns was extended, so was the distance at which engagements would be fought. This meant that ships were increasingly likely to be struck by plunging fire, which would strike a horizontal surface instead of the vertical armour belt. On the plus side, the new ships were fitted with the first-ever torpedo bulkhead to cover the magazine areas. Overall, protection was thought to be adequate for the ships' intended mission and in keeping with Fisher's thinking that speed equalled protection.

SUBSEQUENT BRITISH BATTLECRUISER DESIGNS

The next class of battlecruisers was built as part of the 1908–09 construction programme. Despite the time elapsed from the design of the Invincible class, some three years, the next battlecruiser class demonstrated little improvement. Certainly, these ships did not compare favourably with German ships laid down at the same time. While the plan to build the first ship in the class as a repeat of the *Invincible* design could be understood since the British had inaccurate information on the first German battlecruiser, the decision to proceed with the next two ships of the class to the same dated design was inexcusable. These last two ships were actually paid for by the Dominions they were named for, but they were not laid down until June 1910, which was after the British already had a design for an improved battlecruiser in hand and the details of German construction were much clearer.

The new class, named after lead ship *Indefatigable*, included no difference in the number of weapons in the main and secondary batteries. However, with a longer hull, the placement of the two waist 12in turrets amidships was improved. This resulted in an increased arc of fire on the opposite beam, so that under the right tactical conditions the broadside was increased to eight guns. Placement of the secondary battery of 4in guns was also improved.

The level of armour protection was actually reduced. The maximum depth of the main belt remained at 6in, but the space covered was reduced and the overall weight of the main belt was reduced by almost 100 tons. Protection of the other key areas was largely unchanged, and torpedo protection remained minimal except around the magazines. *Australia* and *New Zealand*, which were laid down well after the lead ship, did feature improved armour arrangements, but possessed the same overall limited protection.

The Royal Navy's next battlecruiser class represented a second-generation design. By 1909, the dreadnought race between Britain and Germany was at a fever pitch. That year, three dreadnoughts and one battlecruiser were approved for the Royal Navy and another three dreadnoughts and another battlecruiser were conditionally approved should their construction be necessary. By August 1909, the second group was approved to counter German construction. More importantly for battlecruiser designers, information had reached the Admiralty that the next class of German battlecruisers was larger than expected. In this light, the early plan to build ships based on the Indefatigable class was quickly scrapped and a clean slate given to the designers. The result was a much better design.

To counter the German battlecruisers, the new British design was much larger, with a displacement increase of 7,600 tons and an additional 110ft in length than *Indefatigable*. In turn, this permitted a heavier main battery of 13.5in guns, which, for the first time, were all placed on the centreline. Protection was also increased, with the main belt increased to a maximum depth of 9in and for the first time, the width of the belt covered the upper decks. Armour protection of other key areas was also increased. More powerful machinery was fitted, which resulted in an increase in speed to 27kt.

The first of the three Indefatigable-class ships was laid down in early 1909 and completed two years later. This Indefatigable-class ship, HMS *New Zealand*, was built for the Royal New Zealand Navy but presented to the Royal Navy on completion in 1912. The double row of portholes indicates that the armour belt did not cover a wide portion of the hull; this combined with the inadequate depth of the belt to leave the ship seriously under-protected. (State Library of South Australia/CC-BY-2.0)

Tiger was the last of the British 13.5in-gunned battlecruisers and the most heavily protected, with 6,598 tons of armour accounting for 25.9 per cent of her normal displacement. Nevertheless, compared to the German Derfflinger class, built at about the same time, *Tiger* remained under-protected. (National Archives of Canada)

The new class was named after the lead ship, *Lion*, and both battlecruisers funded in 1909 were completed to this design. As much of an improvement as *Lion* was over previous classes, it still did not compare favourably with its German contemporaries of the Moltke class even though *Lion* and sister ship *Princess Royal* displaced some 3,710 more tons than *Moltke*. The British ships were slightly faster and were more heavily armed with the new 13.5in gun. However, the German ships remained better protected with a thicker and wider main belt and possessed superior horizontal protection. One of the primary reasons for the continued British deficit in protection was the space requirements for boiler and machinery spaces. The German ships could be reduced in length due to smaller and more efficient propulsion space requirements, and this resulted in a lesser displacement allowing the savings to be used as extra armour.

Repulse was laid down in 1915 and actually represented a step backwards in armoured protection, but she was heavily armed with 15in guns and possessed a maximum speed of almost 32kt. She was extensively modified after completion, as shown here, and survived until World War II, being sunk in 1941. (Cody Images)

The adoption of the 13.5in gun was a major advancement since the new guns were more accurate, possessed greater penetrating power, and presented a total broadside weight almost double that of the 12in-armed battlecruisers. The British finally decided to adopt superfiring turrets, which meant that all guns were placed on the centreline and the inefficient waist turret arrangement was discarded. The weight of the new turrets meant that only four could be fitted. On the other hand, the light 4in secondary battery was retained, but the guns were placed in better locations.

The next battlecruiser was approved in 1910 and laid down in March 1911. The ship was named *Queen Mary*, and since she was begun within months of the preceding Lion-class units, she was essentially a repeat of *Lion*. However, slight modifications placed her into a new class. The armament was unchanged, as was the propulsion system. The principal difference was a minor change in the distribution of the armour.

After *Queen Mary*, only one more battlecruiser was laid down before the war. The 1911 Programme provided funds for a single battlecruiser. Originally, it was intended to build an improved version of *Queen Mary*, but the Admiralty's lead designer proposed a much-improved design which was approved in December 1911.

The new ship, named *Tiger*, incorporated several important improvements. The main battery remained at eight 13.5in guns in four turrets, but the new class introduced a new main battery placement with one of the turrets being moved from a position forward of the third stack to abaft the stack. This gave the turret a larger arc of fire and allowed targets astern to be engaged. The primary difference in armament was the adoption of 6in guns for the secondary battery. By 1912, the British were convinced that massed torpedo attack was a part of German naval doctrine, and the more powerful secondary guns would be better able to counter the torpedo boat threat. Protection was also improved, though the maximum armour depth remained the same, and the additional armour was used to protect more of the ship. To protect the secondary battery and preserve it for when it was needed to ward off attacking

Hood, the last of the British battlecruisers. Redesigned after Jutland, the ship served into World War II. She was lost in May 1941 to a magazine explosion caused by heavy gunfire, thus continuing the debate over protection levels for British battlecruisers. (Allan C. Green/ Adam Cuerden/State Library of Victoria-PD)

15

German torpedo boats, the casemates on the forecastle deck were provided with 6in of armour. The distribution of deck armour was also improved.

The final result was the best British battlecruiser design of the war, but despite increases in protection, the ship still proved vulnerable to heavy shells. When compared to the last pre-war German battlecruisers of the Derfflinger class, *Tiger* was an inferior ship overall.

After *Tiger*, subsequent British battlecruiser designs took a different path, and in any event were not completed in time to see any action against their German counterparts. Fisher returned as First Sea Lord in October 1914 and again pursued his speed-as-armour concept with new energy. The result was the order for a new class of large battlecruisers in early 1915. These were *Repulse* and *Renown* which, though excellent seaboats and fast (capable of more than 31kt), possessed totally inadequate vertical (maximum 6in belt) and horizontal armour. Later in 1915, a class of heavily armed 'large light cruisers' was ordered, which were designed to be suitable for duty in the Baltic. These possessed large guns (18in) but were totally unsuited for fleet work. The final battlecruiser laid down during the war was HMS *Hood*. Ironically, this event took place on the day of the Jutland action when battlecruisers fared so poorly. The lessons of the battle forced her design to be re-cast, and the ship was not completed until 1920. Upon completion, *Hood* was actually a fast battleship. Even this new level of protection proved inadequate, and she was sunk in May 1941 at the hands of a modern battleship.

BATTLECRUISER EMPLOYMENT

The mission of the new armoured cruisers remained the same as the older ships – to provide the fleet with a reconnaissance force heavy and fast enough to fight through enemy screening forces to report on the opposing main fleet. The ships were fast enough that when superior enemy forces were detected, they could disengage at will.

However, this was not how they were used. In 1913, the official title of armoured cruisers became battlecruisers, as appeared more appropriate for a large ship with heavy armament. Seen as capital ships, they were not deployed as their design dictated. Instead of refusing combat with heavy enemy ships, the Royal Navy's battlecruisers used their superior speed to engage the enemy more closely. This practice brought the lightly armoured battlecruisers into tactical situations where their lack of armour was a distinct disadvantage. In particular, the light horizontal armour of the ships was exposed since engagements were taking place at ranges where plunging fire was the primary danger. Thus, the concept of a large cruiser with a dreadnought level of firepower was not a flawed concept in itself; rather the manner in which they were utilized was. Used as large cruisers, they would have been able to outgun any cruiser-sized ship and possessed the speed to decline battle from a more heavily armoured dreadnought. However, the temptation to place a ship with dreadnought-type armament into the battle line proved too great. When used as a fast battleship, the battlecruiser would face the type of warship it was designed to avoid.

Since the British battlecruisers were used as a scouting force, they were employed in advance of the fleet. German battlecruisers were used in an identical manner, which

BRITISH MAIN ARMAMENT

The dual 13.5in/45 gun turret was the main armament for a number of British battleships, but also for battlecruisers *Lion*, *Princess Royal*, *Queen Mary* and *Tiger*. This was a fine weapon, which gave the British battlecruiser a potential edge in firepower over their German counterparts since it possessed greater range and fired a much heavier shell. The gun fired a 1,250lb and a 1,400lb shell; due to shell-hoist arrangements, only *Tiger* could fire the heavier shell. Below the turret were shell-handling rooms, which led down to the magazine. This entire trunk was protected by an armored barbette, which was usually among the most heavily protected parts of the ship.

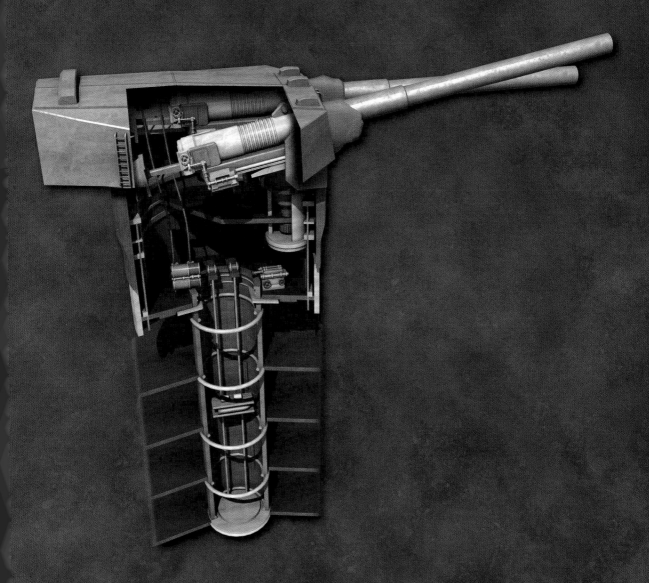

guaranteed that when the battle fleets sought action, the natural enemy of the British battlecruiser was its German counterpart. This brought the more lightly armoured British ships into direct contact with the heavier German ships, with foreseeable consequences.

BRITISH BATTLECRUISER ARMAMENT

The standard main gun for the first six battlecruisers was the 12in/45. These were successful weapons, but not outstanding. Beginning with the Lion class, the British moved up to the 13.5in/45, which possessed a much heavier projectile and therefore much greater hitting power.

Technical characteristics of British battlecruiser guns				
Gun	Weight of shell	Muzzle velocity	Elevation	Range
12in/45 Mk X	851lb	2,725ft/sec	13.5 degrees	18,850yd
13.5in/45 Mk V	1,400lb	2,491ft/sec	20 degrees	23,820yd

Generally, the rate of fire for large British guns was two rounds per minute. Because of slower shell hoists, this was less rapid than the normal German rate of fire.

The British used wire-wound barrels because they were cheaper to produce, but they had less than 40 per cent of the life of the Krupp-manufactured inner-cased barrels. Because the British used increased safety factors, their guns were also much heavier than German ones. The British tended to avoid high muzzle velocities for fear of excessive wear. They were never able to match the Germans' ability to combine high velocity with accuracy.

British battlecruisers enjoyed a potential firepower advantage over their German counterparts. However, this was largely nullified by other factors. British large-calibre shells were unreliable. The capped armour-piercing shells in service at the start of the war had adequate penetrating power against Krupp cemented armour if it struck the target squarely, but when they hit the target obliquely (as was most often the case),

This view of *Tiger* shows the layout of her eight-gun 13.5in main battery in four twin turrets. Though the ship was fitted with a 9in main armour belt, this was still inferior to the best-protected German battlecruisers' armour. (Library of Congress)

British shells tended to break up on impact. Fusing problems meant that when the shells penetrated, they exploded immediately. The bursting agent, Lyddite (picric acid), generally exploded even when it penetrated an armoured plate of only a few inches. In short, British shells were too brittle. New shells with a different shell-cap shape made of a harder steel alloy and with a smaller amount of less sensitive bursting agent were not available until 1917. In addition, British shells had a problem with dispersion. This was traced back to uneven acceleration of the shell inside the barrel as the powder was consumed. This unpredictable ballistic behaviour meant that the shell would not follow the path required to meet fire-control requirements.

Adding to their problems, the British selected Cordite MD (Modified Cordite) as their shell propellant in 1901. This was a nitroglycerin powder and proved to be an unfortunate choice. On the positive side, it caused less barrel corrosion, but this was overshadowed by the tendency of the powder to burn quickly when exposed to fire. The cartridges were carried in a case. These cases were unloaded and then saved, a procedure that could slow down the rate of fire.

Following the first battlecruiser clash at Dogger Bank, the British drew a key lesson. If the rate of fire had been increased, more damage could have been inflicted. To achieve this, handling of charges and shells had to be speeded up. This led to many charges being taken out of their cases and staged at various points outside the magazine. The potential for disaster was clear since flash doors were inadequate in the trunks and hoists and even the magazine doors were not flash-tight – and in the urge to increase the rate of fire, the magazine doors were left open in combat. All of this made British battlecruisers shockingly vulnerable. In fact, it is clear that the primary reason for the loss of three battlecruisers at Jutland was faulty powder and powder-handling procedures rather than the thin armour on the ships.

GERMAN DESIGN PRINCIPLES

The nation most concerned about the British development of the battlecruiser was Germany. By 1906, when the first battlecruiser was laid down, the Germans were locked into a naval race with the British, so there was no doubt that the Germans would meet this latest British challenge. However, the Germans went about building their own battlecruisers in a distinctly different and unhurried way. The Germans did not adopt the term battlecruiser (*Schlachtkreuzer*) until after the war. From their inception until that time, the Germans called their battlecruisers large cruisers (*Grosser Kreuzer*). Like the British, the first large cruiser was an adaptation of the armoured cruiser. The last German armoured cruiser set the pattern for the large cruisers to follow. This was *Blücher*, designed in 1904–05. Compared to other armoured cruisers of the day, she was among the fastest, was the most heavily armoured (7in of belt armour), but carried a relatively small main battery of 8.2in guns. Though she was a fine armoured cruiser, she was already totally outclassed by the Royal Navy's new Invincible class.

When it came to following the British changes to the size and firepower of the armoured cruiser, the Germans had to wait to see what developed before responding.

Because the plan for the Invincible class had been prepared under conditions of secrecy, all the Germans knew was that the 1905 Naval Programme included the consideration for the construction of four new armoured cruisers. In 1906, the Germans were assuming that these new ships were in the 16,000-ton range and were each armed with eight 9.2in guns. This was soon clarified with information that the new ships were in fact 17,500 tons and had an unprecedented speed of 25kt. In response, the Germans planned to build an updated armoured cruiser of 15,000 tons with an even higher speed of 26kt but with the relatively light armament of 12 8.2in guns. No sooner had construction begun on this ship, named *Blücher*, than the full story of *Invincible*'s design became known. Not only did the British ships possess great speed, but each was armed with an all-big-gun battery of 12in guns. The Germans quickly decided to follow suit.

Design work on the first German large cruiser began in August 1906 after the characteristics of *Invincible* were known. The adoption of steam-turbine propulsion brought speed close to British standards even on a higher displacement. The adoption of a smaller and thus lighter main battery allowed more weight to be used for armour. The result was a better-balanced design. From the first German battlecruiser, protection was superior to their British counterparts and even in some cases comparable to early British dreadnoughts.

The Germans, led by chief designer Hans Bürkner, were tasked by the Secretary of State for the Imperial Naval Office, Admiral Alfred von Tirpitz (1849–1930), with improving the quality of German capital ships. Even as the German naval budget was stretched to the limit to keep up with the British, funds were made available for prolonged testing of new concepts and equipment. The result was that German ships were more thoroughly designed than British ones. This was proven by the fact that German designs devoted less weight to hull and machinery. In turn, this allowed the incorporation of greater armour to protect greater areas of the ship. In addition, Bürkner placed great emphasis on providing underwater protection. To minimize damage from torpedoes and mines, the Germans incorporated an anti-torpedo defence system, which featured a torpedo bulkhead. In front of that was a void that could be as deep as 13ft. Half of the space was filled with coal and the other half left empty. This system proved largely successful against World War I mines and torpedoes. The incorporation of a dedicated anti-torpedo system required that German ships have a larger beam. This provided the side benefit of increased stability in general and being a more stable gun platform. A second layer of underwater protection was provided by an extensive system of compartmentation in an attempt to limit any flooding should the anti-torpedo system be broached. British battlecruisers had no dedicated torpedo protection except over their magazines.

It is clear that German battlecruiser designs favoured protection over firepower and speed. Generally, the British placed protection third in the trio of design priorities. While British ships were generally faster than their German counterparts, the margin was usually small. Firepower was another story, and German capital ships can accurately be said to be under-armed. However, this gap was less than it appeared given inferior British shell design and bursting charges. Since British battlecruisers were generally under-protected, even the smaller German main guns had few problems penetrating their armour at normal ranges.

GERMAN BATTLECRUISER DESIGNS

Design work began on the first German battlecruiser in August 1906 and the ship was laid down in March 1908. Named *Von der Tann*, it was completed in early 1911. Since the ship was a direct response to *Invincible*, a comparison of the two classes is revealing. *Von der Tann* was much better protected with a 10in main belt compared to *Invincible*'s 6in of armour. Turrets were better armoured and the casemates on the German ship also received 6in of armour. Total weight of armour was 5,693 tons compared to some 3,735 tons on *Invincible*. The armament of the first German battlecruiser was eight 11in guns mounted in four turrets. The forward and aft turrets were placed on the centreline, but the waist turrets had a restricted arc of fire. Contrary to the British practice, the starboard waist turret was always forward of the port waist turret. They were also placed more inboard than on British ships. They could conduct fire on the opposite beam, but only on a 125-degree arc. The secondary battery was much heavier than that on *Invincible* with ten 5.9in guns and 16 3.5in guns mounted in casemates.

Armoured protection of *Von der Tann* was adequate against the 12in British gun. The main belt reached a maximum depth of 10in, but this was tapered down to 4.75in at the bow and to 4in just short of the stern. Unlike on British ships, the secondary battery located in casemates was protected by 6in of armour. Other key areas like the turret barbettes and the face of the 11in turrets were given 9in of armour and the conning tower had 10in. The ship was given a dedicated torpedo defensive system that extended the same length of the main belt, that is from the area of the forward turret to the area of the aft turret.

The next large cruiser was the Moltke class. Unlike the British, who made no real improvements from their first to their second class of battlecruiser, the Moltke class presented real upgrades from the Von der Tann class. The new class was heavier by some 3,800 tons and longer by 45ft, which allowed the placement of heavier armour and additional guns. For the layout of the main battery, the designers referred to the Kaiser-class dreadnoughts, which included an additional 11in gun turret aft placed in a superfiring position. The Germans decided to retain the 11in guns instead of moving

Moltke was the lead ship of the second generation of German battlecruisers, entering service in 1912. The ship was clearly superior to contemporary British battlecruiser designs. (Library of Congress)

Seydlitz pictured before the war. This view shows the heightened forecastle and the starboard-side waist 11in gun turret. The elaborate and impractical system to deploy a torpedo net is also clearly visible. (NHHC NH 46839)

up to the 12in guns that were now standard on their dreadnoughts. However, the new 11in/50 gun was fitted. Armour was increased to a maximum of 11in on the belt, which was almost as heavy as those of British dreadnoughts being built at the same time and far superior to those of the British battlecruisers then being constructed.

The 1910 programme included authorization for an improved *Moltke*. This ship, named *Seydlitz*, possessed refinements to increase her seakeeping characteristics and speed. Retaining the same firepower and protection, the vessel's primary difference was to add another deck to the forecastle. Since German ships were designed for operations primarily in the North Sea and not the open Atlantic, endurance and seakeeping were usually secondary considerations. *Seydlitz* also carried more powerful machinery and this, combined with a hull possessing a reduced beam and an additional 46ft in length, increased top speed to 26.5kt.

The third generation of German large cruisers resulted in the best battlecruiser design to see combat during the war. The three ships of the Derfflinger class possessed the best protection of any battlecruiser completed during the war and were comparable to almost all British dreadnoughts. The layout of the main battery was new. The eight-gun battery was comprised of 12in guns, the only German large cruiser so equipped. The four turrets were placed in pairs, forward and aft. The addition of two superfiring turrets increased topweight, so the new class had a lower freeboard, which detracted from its seakeeping capabilities. The ships were given another first, a flush main deck with a rising sheer forward. The ships were also the only German large cruisers to be fitted with a tripod mast, though these were installed in 1916 after Jutland. Another innovation was in the ship's

Seydlitz was the most heavily damaged German battlecruiser of the war. The toughness of its design was demonstrated by the fact that the ship survived severe damage at Dogger Bank and Jutland and a mine explosion in April 1916. (Cody Images)

machinery. Of her 18 boilers, four were oil-fired. This gave the ship an increased range over the previous class. Even with a greater displacement, the Derfflinger class reached 28kt in service. The third ship of the class, *Hindenburg*, did not reach the fleet until after Jutland. She was slightly different from the first two ships in the class, with a slightly longer hull and more powerful machinery designed to give her an extra knot in speed.

GERMAN LARGE CRUISER ARMAMENT

The Germans preferred smaller main guns with higher muzzle velocities. They did not believe that a long-range weapon was necessary since visibility conditions in the expected battleground of the North Sea militated against long-range duels. The Germans believed that a smaller weapon would have a greater rate of fire than a heavier gun and they also liked the ballistic properties of the 11in gun and thought this gun compared well to the standard British 12in gun. Nevertheless, they undoubtedly waited too long to move beyond the trusted 11in gun as the British were already placing 13.5in guns in their battlecruisers by the time the Germans finally went to the 12in gun. The German selection of main guns translated into superior engagement ranges for the British battlecruisers equipped with the 13.5in gun.

Technical characteristics of German battlecruiser weapons				
Gun	Weight of shell	Muzzle velocity	Elevation	Range
11in/45	666lb	2,805ft/sec	20 degrees	22,000yd
11in/50	666lb	2,887ft/sec	13.5/16 degrees	19,500yd/21,000yd
12in/50	893lb	2,805ft/sec	13.5/16 degrees	20,500yd/22,400yd

The 11in/45 gun (actually 11.14in) was mounted on *Von der Tann*. The improved 11in/50 gun was on the Moltke class and *Seydlitz*. The 12in guns were placed on the Derfflinger class. The loading cycle for these was 20 seconds. Following Dogger Bank,

This pre-war view of *Moltke* shows the ship's main difference from the preceding Von der Tann class – the addition of another 11in/50 gun turret aft. Based on the experience of Dogger Bank, the maximum elevation of these turrets was increased to 16 degrees before Jutland to increase the 11in gun's maximum range. (Library of Congress)

23

GERMAN MAIN ARMAMENT

The dual 11in/50 gun turret was the primary armament on the two ships of the Moltke class and the unique *Seydlitz*. The Germans preferred the lighter 11in gun for a number of reasons, and while the weapon was comparable to the 12in gun aboard the first-generation British battlecruisers, it was outclassed by the 13.5in weapon on the latest British battlecruisers. The face of the gun turret was one of the most heavily armoured places on the ship — 9in on *Moltke* and *Goeben* and 10in on *Seydlitz*. Since the prospects for striking the turret on its side and top were judged to be less likely, these were much less heavily armoured. The Germans heavily protected the barbette below the turret, but did not ensure the areas between the handling areas and the magazine were flash tight.

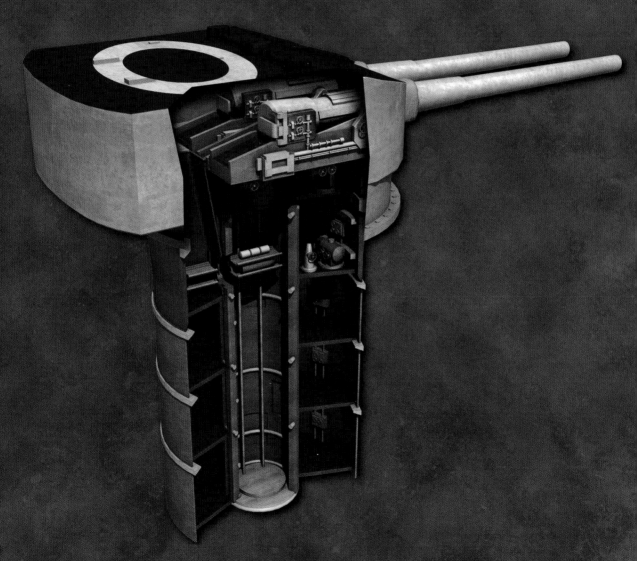

the turret mountings of German guns were modified to permit greater elevation. The increased elevations resulted in greater ranges.

The secondary battery of German battlecruisers consisted of 5.9in guns mounted in single guns in casemates. These were intended to engage capital ships. German battlecruisers also carried large numbers of 3.5in guns for engaging enemy torpedo boats and destroyers. Many of these were mounted in casemates, and some of them were located low in the hull or well forward, which made them unworkable in any kind of sea. Secondary guns could fire up to seven rounds per minute.

In addition to the excellence of their Krupp-produced guns, the Germans produced high-quality shells. The Germans had developed a delayed-action fuse for their large shells, which meant that the shells exploded inside the ship. This meant that German shells could penetrate to the vitals of a ship and cause much greater damage.

GERMAN CHARGE-HANDLING PROCEDURES

The characteristics of German powder were another key advantage. Charges were carried in two parts. The main charge came in a brass cartridge and a smaller one in a metal case. The brass cartridges increased the weight of the ammunition, but protected against handling accidents caused by sparks and increased barrel life. The use of metal cartridges meant the Germans believed that a lesser degree of anti-flash protection in the magazines and handling areas was necessary. This meant that magazines were kept open even during action. The shorter length of the German charge when compared to British charges also helped the Germans achieve a higher rate of fire. The most important characteristic of German powder charges was that when hit, they tended to burn, but not to explode. Obviously, this had devastating results for the immediate area of the fire, but since there was no violent explosion, the entire ship was not imperilled.

The importance of this was shown by the damage to *Seydlitz* at Dogger Bank. The ship was penetrated at long range by a British 13.5in shell in the area of the rear gun turret. The shell penetrated the deck armour and hit the turret barbette sending hot fragments from the armour into the shell-handling room where over 13,000lb of powder was located. However, only the fore-charges in their thin zinc cases actually ignited, while the charges in the heavier brass cases did not. The magazine was flooded before the larger charges or the shells were ignited. The resulting fire killed the crew of the turret and even spread to the adjacent turret, but there was no explosion. A similar incident on a British ship would have resulted in its destruction.

This experience led to changes in German charge-handling procedures. The number of charges in the handling room and working chamber was decreased. When the same thing happened again on *Seydlitz* at Jutland, the charges once more ignited, but since there were fewer of them, the fire was restricted to the handling room and working chamber. The Germans did not take any additional flash precautions before Jutland since they judged that limiting the number of charges out of the magazine would be sufficient.

THE STRATEGIC SITUATION

On 4 August 1914, Great Britain declared war on Germany. Many thought that the clash of the British and German navies in the North Sea would follow shortly thereafter. This mindset was the result of the heated naval rivalry between the two powers and the German expectation that the Royal Navy would institute a close blockade of the principal German naval bases in the North Sea. However, the advent of the mine, torpedo and submarine made such an undertaking extremely hazardous. In addition, the blockading force could potentially be subject to a sudden and overwhelming attack from the German fleet. By 1912, the British had jettisoned the idea of a close blockade in favour of what was called an 'observational' blockade. This also proved impossible since it required excessive numbers of small fleet units. When war finally came, the observational blockade had been replaced with a distant blockade. This removed the possibility of an immediate clash with the Kaiserliche Marine (Imperial German Navy) since the main British fleet, named the Grand Fleet, was positioned at the base of Scapa Flow in the Orkney Islands off the Scottish coast. The Grand Fleet was frequently at sea patrolling the exit from the North Sea, but at a respectable distance from the German bases along the North Sea.

The Germans also realized that the British would have a difficult time imposing and maintaining a close blockade, but they still expected this to happen when the war began. The German plan going into the war was to use submarines, destroyers and mines to attack the light British forces they expected to be operating in close proximity to their bases. The British would be forced to support these forces, thus affording the opportunity to reduce overall British strength to a point where the German fleet could engage under favourable conditions.

As it turned out, when war began the Germans were caught by surprise by the British adoption of the distant-blockade strategy. Since there was no question of sending the fleet to the northern North Sea to engage the much larger Grand Fleet, this meant that the Germans had no effective naval strategy. Thus a situation developed where the antagonists eyed each other warily from opposite ends of the North Sea while both sides resorted to minelaying and submarine attacks.

The British battlecruisers operated out of an anchorage at Cromarty Firth on the east coast of Scotland. These were under the command of Rear-Admiral David Beatty (1871–1936). By August, the inertia of inaction was too much to bear for the commanders of the Royal Navy's light forces. The Admiralty approved a plan in late August for two flotillas of destroyers supported by submarines to attack German patrols in the Heligoland Bight off the German fortress of Heligoland Island. Immediate support was provided by the battlecruisers *Invincible* and *New Zealand* just to the north. The Grand Fleet was not kept well informed about the operation, but Beatty's battlecruiser force was committed at the last second, without the knowledge of the British light forces.

On 28 August, the British began their sweep. The battle was fought in conditions of haze and fog. The British destroyer flotillas were under increasing pressure as German cruisers arrived from their nearby bases. Their request for support was heard by Beatty some 40 miles away. In what became his typical response to all situations, Beatty decided to rush into action in spite of the danger of submarines, mines or even German capital ships that could already have departed their bases. The battlecruisers faced these potential threats in conditions of low visibility. On this occasion, Beatty's gamble was rewarded. Three German light cruisers were sunk and the first naval clash of the war was a British victory.

Such a relatively minor clash had major implications for the Germans. The British had ventured close to the German base on Heligoland, and the German response was found wanting. The British victory heightened the defensive mindset of the Germans. Most importantly, the Kaiser ordered that if the commander of the Hochseeflotte (High Seas Fleet), Admiral Friedrich von Ingenohl (1857–1933), wanted to commit his fleet to action, he had to secure the Kaiser's approval.

Both sides were becoming increasingly restless about the lack of apparent action in the North Sea. Unknown to the Germans, the British margin of superiority was eroding. One British dreadnought was lost to a mine in October, and several others were experiencing engine problems that temporarily forced them out of service. The battlecruiser situation was even more serious for the British. At the battle of Coronel off the Chilean coast on 1 November, a German squadron led by two armoured cruisers defeated a British squadron. In response, the battlecruisers *Invincible* and *Inflexible* were dispatched to chase down the German cruisers and battlecruiser *Princess Royal* was sent to guard the northern entrance of the Panama Canal. Also in November, Turkey entered the war and battlecruisers *Indomitable* and *Indefatigable* were retained in the Mediterranean to watch the German battlecruiser *Goeben*, which had taken refuge in Turkey. This meant that only *Lion*, *Queen Mary* and *New Zealand*, plus the newly commissioned and not fully ready *Tiger*, were available in the North Sea. The Germans had four battlecruisers, which resulted in no advantage for the British. In January 1915, *Derfflinger* joined the German fleet.

Units of the High Seas Fleet during an operation in the North Sea in 1916. After Scheer assumed command, the Germans were much more aggressive and actively sought an engagement under favourable conditions. (IWM HU 58253)

In an effort to increase the effect of attrition upon British forces, the Germans had decided in early October to increase minelaying along the British coast and to use their battlecruisers to bombard British towns. The joint minelaying and bombardment operations were intended to draw part of the Grand Fleet over a newly laid minefield or into a group of U-boats. The first bombardment was conducted on 3 November against Yarmouth. Damage ashore was light, and losses to the Royal Navy negligible, but the British were forced to take measures to increase the defences of the eastern coast, and the Germans were encouraged enough to try a similar operation.

The next operation was delayed until December because of problems with one of the German battlecruisers' machinery. The Germans were anxious to conduct the operation before the return of the two British battlecruisers known to be in the South Atlantic, which had destroyed the German cruiser squadron at the battle of the Falkland Islands on 8 December. This time, the battlecruiser bombardment and minelaying operation would be supported by the entire High Seas Fleet, which would come halfway across the North Sea into the area known as Dogger Bank.

At this point, the developing British advantage in signals intelligence has to be mentioned. On the first floor of the old Admiralty building, the Royal Navy had established a code-breaking organization known as Room 40. After a difficult beginning stemming from inexperience and excessive secrecy, Room 40 began to make enough headway that it could provide warning of forthcoming German operations. No warning was provided of the Yarmouth raid, but for the next German raid in December, Room 40 was able to provide warning to the Grand Fleet that something was up. Unfortunately for the British, on this occasion, Room 40 was only able to discern part of the operation and the British remained ignorant that the entire High Seas Fleet intended to go to sea to support the battlecruisers. This could have led to disaster since the British only planned to deploy six dreadnoughts from the Grand Fleet to support Beatty's battlecruisers, which would intercept the Germans on their way back to base. In fact, the High Seas Fleet would only be some 30 miles from the intended meeting point for Beatty and the single battle squadron from the Grand Fleet. This was the perfect opportunity for the Germans to destroy a detached element of the Grand Fleet and even the overall naval balance in the North Sea.

The actual raid on 16 December held surprises for both sides. The German battlecruisers bombarded Scarborough, Whitby and Hartlepool, inflicting heavy damage and civilian casualties, and an accompanying light cruiser successfully laid a minefield. Both sides were unable to capitalize upon favourable tactical situations due to the poor visibility. The British actually made contact with the light cruiser screen covering the German battlecruisers, but neither Beatty nor the dreadnoughts from the Grand Fleet were able to engage the German battlecruisers. For their part, the Germans also let an opportunity slip away when the screen of the High Seas Fleet clashed with the destroyers from the detached squadron of the Grand Fleet. Though only some 10 miles away, Ingenohl turned away thinking that the entire Grand Fleet was present.

For the next operation, the Germans decided to conduct a raid out to the Dogger Bank area. The Germans believed that British light forces were present there, and they wanted to verify their suspicion that the numerous fishing trawlers in the rich fishing grounds of the Dogger Bank were not British scouts reporting the activities of raiding German forces. On 23 January, Room 40 decoded the orders to the German battlecruisers to conduct the Dogger Bank operation the following day. The first battlecruiser duel was at hand.

TECHNICAL SPECIFICATIONS

BRITISH BATTLECRUISERS

INVINCIBLE CLASS

The three ships of the Invincible class were ordered under the 1905–06 programme and were laid down in early 1906. The efficient British shipyards of the day launched them about a year later, but the ships were not completed until October 1908 (*Indomitable* and *Inflexible*) and March 1909 (*Invincible*).

The main battery comprised eight 12in guns in four turrets. These were arranged so that the two waist turrets fitted amidships could conduct cross-deck firing on their opposite beam. This was done in the ship's first engagement at the Falklands Islands, but the damage to the deck and the shock to the crew of the other waist turret meant that it was decided that this would only be done again in an emergency. This limited the broadside for the rest of the war to six guns. The secondary battery consisted of the inadequate 4in gun; 16 were fitted originally in single mounts, but this was reduced to 12 in 1915. Five torpedo tubes were carried, four broadside and one in the stern.

The demands for a heavy armament, high speed, and a great range from a high fuel capacity and superior endurance from high freeboard, meant that designers had to sacrifice somewhere. This was in the area of protection. The main belt armour was 6in deep and extended from the area of the forward turret back to the aft turret. The turret barbettes were slightly more armoured at 7in, as were the face, sides and rear of the turrets themselves. The forward conning tower was given a maximum of 10in of armour. The deck armour had a maximum thickness of 2in and most of the ship was covered by less than that. There was no special torpedo protection aside from additional longitudinal protection for the magazines.

The machinery provided power for speed greater than the 25kt design speed. On trials, all three ships exceeded 26kt. The 31 boilers drove four turbines. Even at this speed, these were the slowest British battlecruisers, which proved a tactical disadvantage during the war.

All three ships saw extensive action during the war. At the battle of the Falkland Islands, *Invincible* and *Inflexible* proved that when employed correctly, they could perform well. In an action against two German armoured cruisers, the battlecruisers used their 12in guns to destroy both German ships while incurring insignificant damage in return. *Indomitable* fought at Dogger Bank. *Inflexible* survived a mine explosion in March 1915. All three ships were assigned to the Grand Fleet at Jutland, where *Invincible* was sunk. The surviving two ships saw no further combat action and were sold for scrap in 1921.

Invincible class	
Ships in class:	*Inflexible, Indomitable, Invincible*
Displacement (normal):	17,290–17,420 tons
Dimensions:	Length 567ft; beam 78ft 8in; draught 25ft 1in
Armament:	Eight 12in/45 guns; 16 4in guns; five 18in torpedo tubes
Protection:	Main belt: 6in (maximum); deck 2.5in (maximum); turrets 7in (face), 7in (sides), 3in (top); conning tower 10in (face), 7in (rear); barbettes 7in. Total weight of armour: 3,460 tons
Machinery:	Four Parsons turbines driving four shafts; 31 boilers creating 46,500shp (shaft horsepower); top speed 26.6kt
Range:	6,210nm (nautical miles) at 10kt
Crew:	781–799 (1914)

INDEFATIGABLE CLASS

The next class of British battlecruisers offered only a slight improvement on the Invincible class. The main battery remained eight 12in guns, but the two waist turrets were arranged to allow cross-deck firing to the opposite beam, thus creating an increased broadside. The secondary battery still consisted of the 4in gun, but the placement of the guns was improved.

Most surprisingly, the Invincible class's biggest issue, its lack of protection, remained unaddressed. In fact, the overall weight of the main belt actually decreased and the overall layout of the armour was inferior. Put simply, the two classes that made up the first generation of British battlecruisers were inferior ships to their first-generation German counterparts. While both sides possessed roughly similar firepower and speed,

INDEFATIGABLE CLASS

Ships in class:	*Indefatigable*, *New Zealand*, *Australia*
Displacement (normal):	18,750 tons
Dimensions:	Length 590ft; beam 79ft 10in; draught 26ft 3in
Armament:	Eight 12in/45 guns; 16 4in guns; two 18in torpedo tubes
Protection:	Main belt 6in (maximum); deck 2.5in (maximum); turrets 7in (face), 7in (sides), 3in (top); conning tower 10in; barbettes 7in. Total weight of armour: 3,735 tons
Machinery:	Four Parsons turbines driving four shafts; 31 boilers creating 55,880shp; top speed 26.9kt
Range:	6,690nm at 10kt
Crew:	790–818 (1913)

OPPOSITE: HMS *NEW ZEALAND*

New Zealand as completed in 1912, one of the three ships of the Indefatigable class. These battlecruisers were essentially a repeat of the Invincible class. Clearly visible is the main battery of eight 12in guns in four turrets. What is not evident is the inadequate level of protection, which made all first-generation British battlecruisers inferior to their German counterparts.

the Germans managed to add considerably more protection. While *Indefatigable* mounted 3,735 tons of armour, accounting for 19.9 per cent of the ship's normal displacement, *Von der Tann* possessed 5,693 tons of armour, which made up 29.8 per cent of normal displacement.

Indefatigable was destroyed at Jutland in her first engagement. *Australia* missed both Dogger Bank and Jutland, and was scuttled off Sydney in 1924. *New Zealand* spent her career in the North Sea and took part in Dogger Bank and Jutland. She was sold for scrap in 1922.

LION CLASS

The Lion class was the first second-generation British battlecruiser. The lead ship of the class was laid down in late 1909 and completed in May 1912. Her sister ship, *Princess Royal*, was not begun until May 1910 and entered service in November 1912.

This fine view of *New Zealand* clearly shows that the class was a repeat of the Invincible class. Minor improvements in her armoured protection arrangement are not evident, but the fact remains she was markedly inferior to German battlecruisers being built at the same time. (Cody Images)

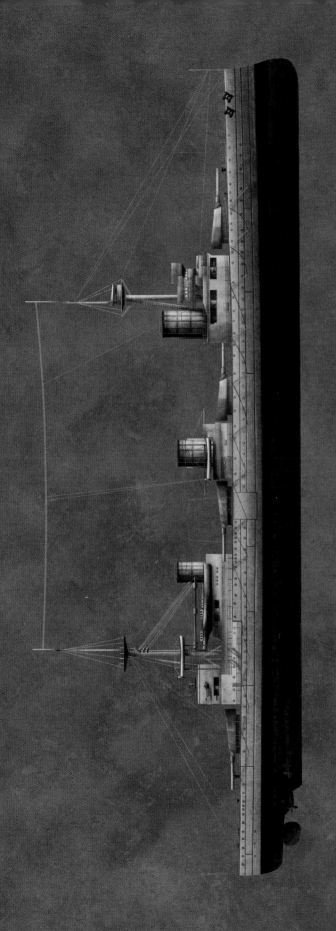

This view is of *Queen Mary* before the war. Clearly visible is the much better arrangement of her main battery, featuring two 13.5in gun turrets forward, and the single amidships turret, which allowed an eight-gun broadside. (IWM Q 21661A)

Dramatic advancements were incorporated in firepower, protection and speed. Most impressively, the new ships were fitted with the new 13.5in gun, with four turrets placed in pairs forward and aft and with the second turret in a superfiring position. The unfortunate choice of the 4in gun as the secondary battery was continued.

The ships' protection was also greatly increased. The main belt was increased by 50 per cent to a maximum of 9in and for the first time an upper belt was fitted, which had a maximum thickness of 6in. Barbette and frontal turret armour was also increased. On completion, the ships possessed the highest speed of any cruiser type afloat. On trials, *Princess Royal* developed an impressive 78,803shp and a maximum speed of 28.5kt.

Both ships were bulwarks of the Battlecruiser Fleet during the war. Both were present at Dogger Bank and Jutland. With the signing of the Washington Naval Treaty in 1922, both were quickly placed on the disposal list and scrapped in 1923–24.

QUEEN MARY CLASS

The 1910 programme included provisions for a single battlecruiser. This ship, named *Queen Mary*, was essentially a repeat of the *Lion* with the exception of some slight increases in horizontal protection and differences in armour arrangements, which provided the secondary battery limited protection and armoured the torpedo control tower. Otherwise, firepower and speed remained unchanged.

The ship was laid down in March 1911 and was handed over to the Royal Navy in August 1913. The ship was in refit in early 1915 and missed the Dogger Bank action. At Jutland, *Queen Mary* was sunk with the loss of all but nine of her crew.

Queen Mary class	
Ships in class:	*Queen Mary*
Displacement (normal):	26,780 tons
Dimensions:	Length 703ft 6in; beam 89ft; draught 28ft
Armament:	Eight 13.5in/45 guns; 16 4in guns; two 21in torpedo tubes
Protection:	Main belt 9in (maximum); deck 2in (maximum); turrets 9in (face), 9in (sides), 3.25in (top); conning tower 10in; barbettes 9in. Total weight of armour: 5,140 tons
Machinery:	Four Parsons turbines driving four shafts; 42 boilers creating 83,450shp; top speed 28.5kt
Range:	5,610nm at 10kt
Crew:	1,275 (1916)

TIGER CLASS

The finest British battlecruiser to see action during the war and the last of the pre-war designs was the single-ship Tiger class. As part of the 1911 programme, *Tiger* was laid down in June 1912, but did not reach the fleet until after the start of the war, in October 1914. Even then, she was rushed into service and was not fully worked up, as her poor performance at Dogger Bank suggests.

Tiger was the first British battlecruiser to carry an adequate secondary armament, 12 6in guns in casemates. This mirrored the secondary armament then being given to dreadnoughts and reflected the heightened concern with the torpedo threat from German torpedo boats. The main battery remained the same as the previous two classes, but a better placement of the turrets resulted in a better arc of fire for 'Q' turret (the turret abaft the aft stack). Armour protection was increased, primarily for the secondary battery. The ship exceeded its design speed and worked up to an impressive 29kt.

The Royal Navy considered *Tiger* a successful design and one of its more graceful ships. She was assigned to the Battlecruiser Fleet for her entire wartime career and saw action at both Dogger Bank and Jutland. She survived the cuts to the Royal Navy's capital ship fleet after the Washington Naval Treaty and remained in service until 1931; she was sold for scrap the following year.

This fine port quarter view shows *Princess Royal* in 1914. Commissioned in 1912, she was the second Lion-class ship to be completed. The ship fought at both Dogger Bank and Jutland. (Cody Images)

LION CLASS

Ships in class:	*Lion, Princess Royal*
Displacement (normal):	26,350 tons
Dimensions:	Length 700ft; beam 88ft 7in; draught 28ft
Armament:	Eight 13.5in/45 guns; 16 4in guns; two 21in torpedo tubes
Protection:	Main belt 9in (maximum); deck 2in (maximum); turrets 9in (face), 9in (sides), 3.25in (top); conning tower 10in; barbettes 9in. Total weight of armour: 5,140 tons
Machinery:	Four Parsons turbines driving four shafts; 42 boilers creating 78,803shp; top speed 28.5kt
Range:	5,610nm at 10kt
Crew:	1,092 (1915)

OPPOSITE: HMS *PRINCESS ROYAL*

Princess Royal as she appeared in 1916 at Jutland. As a second-generation British battlecruiser design, she featured better armour protection and a 13.5in main gun battery. The arrangement of the main battery was also improved, as is evident in this view.

Tiger class	
Ships in class:	*Tiger*
Displacement (normal):	28,800 tons
Dimensions:	Length 704ft 6in; beam 90ft 6in; draught 28ft 3in
Armament:	Eight 13.5in/45 guns; 12 6in guns; two 3in guns; four 21in torpedo tubes
Protection:	Main belt 9in (maximum); deck 3in (maximum); turrets 9in (face), 9in (sides), 3.25in (top); conning tower 10in; barbettes 9in. Total weight of armour: 7,390 tons
Machinery:	Four Brown Curtis turbines driving four shafts; 39 boilers creating 108,000shp; top speed 29kt
Range:	5,200nm at 12kt
Crew:	1,344 (1915)

GERMAN BATTLECRUISERS

VON DER TANN CLASS

The first German battlecruiser was ordered under the 1907–08 construction programme. The single ship of the class was built at the Blohm und Voss shipyard in Hamburg (the builder of all but two of the German battlecruisers) and was completed in 1911, some three years after the British placed their first battlecruiser in service.

Von der Tann had an active career and survived the war. As part of Hipper's battlecruiser squadron, she participated in all of the early-war raids. *Von der Tann* was

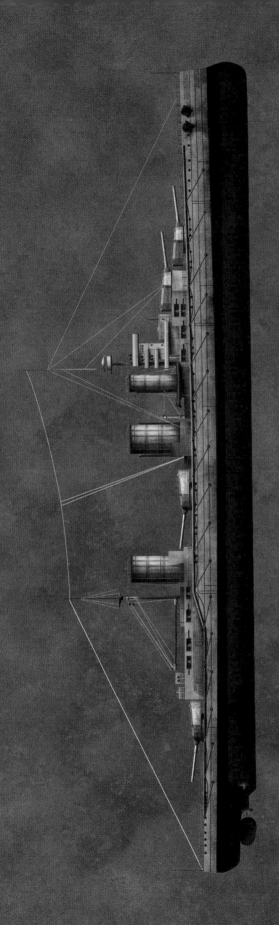
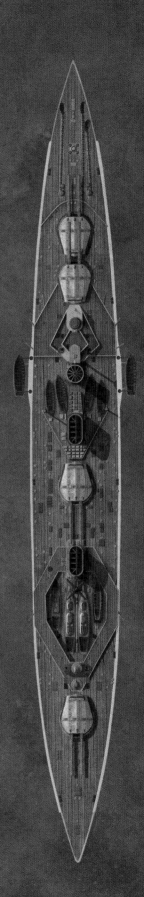

Von der Tann shown shortly after completion in 1911. The view shows the layout of the ship's four 11in gun turrets. Despite being a first-generation battlecruiser, Von der Tann proved a successful design; she fought at Dogger Bank and Jutland and survived the war. (Library of Congress)

undergoing refit in early 1915 and missed the first battlecruiser action at Dogger Bank. She returned in time for Jutland and played a key role sinking *Indefatigable*. She was surrendered at the end of the war and scuttled in June 1919 with most of the rest of the interned High Seas Fleet. The wreck was raised in 1930 and later broken up at Rosyth in 1934.

Von der Tann class	
Ships in class:	*Von der Tann*
Displacement (normal):	19,064 tons
Dimensions:	Length 563ft; beam 87ft; draught 26ft 7in
Armament:	Eight 11in/45 guns; ten 5.9in guns; 16 3.5in guns; four 17.7in torpedo tubes
Protection:	Main belt 10in (maximum); turrets up to 9in (face), 7in (sides), 3.5in (top); conning tower 10in (maximum); barbettes 9in; torpedo bulkhead 2in. Total weight of armour: 5,693 tons
Machinery:	Four Parsons turbines driving four shafts; 18 boilers creating 43,600shp (design[1]); top speed 26.8kt (28kt with sprayed oil)
Range:	4,400nm at 14kt
Crew:	923 (1914; later 1,170)

MOLTKE CLASS

The second class of German battlecruisers represented an improvement of *Von der Tann*, primarily in the area of firepower. By increasing the ship's overall size, a fifth turret was added for a 25 per cent increase in the main battery. This fifth turret was added aft in a superfiring position. The guns themselves were the more powerful 11in/50 model

---

1. This was the designed output of the machinery. However, as with all German ships with turbines, the turbines could be overloaded and shaft horsepower increased.

Goeben was basically an enlarged *Von der Tann* with an additional 11in turret placed aft in a superfiring position, as shown here in this pre-war view. (Cody Images)

compared to *Von der Tann*'s 11in/45. Armour protection was increased slightly. The dramatic increase in displacement translated to a lower top speed of 25.5kt.

The two ships of the class, *Moltke* and *Goeben*, were also built at Hamburg at Blohm und Voss and both entered service in 1912. The design proved very satisfactory in service and both had successful careers. *Moltke* was a stalwart member of Hipper's squadron and survived the war. Surrendered at the end of the war, she was scuttled in 1919, raised in 1927 and scrapped in 1929.

Goeben had the longest career and arguably the greatest impact of any battlecruiser. The start of the war found her in the Mediterranean. Unable to return to Germany, the ship evaded British attempts to intercept her and arrived in Turkey in August 1914. Upon arrival, the ship was nominally transferred to the Turkish Navy and played a prominent role of bringing Turkey into the war. *Goeben* saw extensive service in the Black Sea against the Russian Navy and survived the war. Abandoned, but not scrapped, she was brought back into service and ultimately survived until 1973, finally being scrapped in 1974.

Moltke class	
Ships in class:	*Moltke* and *Goeben*
Displacement (normal):	22,800 tons
Dimensions:	Length 612ft; beam 97ft; draught 29ft 6in
Armament:	Ten 11in/50 guns; 12 5.9in guns; 12 3.5in guns; four 19.7in torpedo tubes
Protection:	Main belt 10.75in (maximum); deck 2in; turrets up to 9in (face and rear), 7in (sides), 3.5in (top); conning tower 14in (maximum); barbettes 9in; torpedo bulkhead 2in. Total weight of armour: 7,600 tons
Machinery:	Four Parsons turbines driving four shafts; 24 boilers creating 52,000shp (design); top speed 25.5kt
Range:	4,120nm at 14kt
Crew:	1,050 (in 1914; by 1916, 1,355)

SEYDLITZ CLASS

Ships in class:	*Seydlitz*
Displacement (normal):	24,320 tons
Dimensions:	Length 658ft; beam 93ft 6in; draught 30ft
Armament:	Ten 11in/50 guns; 12 5.9in guns; 12 3.5in guns; four 19.7in torpedo tubes
Protection:	Main belt 12in (maximum); deck 3.2in; turrets up to 10in (face), 8in (sides), 4in (top); conning tower 14in (maximum); barbettes 9in; torpedo bulkhead 2in. Total weight of armour: not known
Machinery:	Four Parsons turbines driving four shafts; 27 boilers creating 63,000shp (design); top speed 26.5kt
Range:	4,200nm at 14kt
Crew:	1,050 (1914; 1,425 in 1916)

OPPOSITE: SMS *SEYDLITZ*

Seydlitz, entering service in 1913, was the last of the second generation of German battlecruisers. Based on the preceding Moltke class, the ship possessed a main battery of ten 11in guns arranged in five turrets. In an effort to improve seakeeping, the ship received an additional deck on the forecastle.

Goeben was the sister ship of *Moltke*, but never served in northern waters during World War I. She was nominally turned over to the Turkish Navy in 1914, and served in that capacity until 1973. *Goeben* missed the battles of Dogger Bank and Jutland, but had an active career countering Russian forces in the Black Sea. (Cody Images)

SEYDLITZ CLASS

The next development in German battlecruiser design was the single-ship Seydlitz class. The *Seydlitz* continued the basic appearance of the preceding Moltke class, but featured several incremental improvements. The layout and number of guns in the ship's main battery remained unchanged. The main visual difference was the addition of a short forecastle deck, which was an attempt to improve seakeeping and performance at high speeds. This practice was not continued in the next class, probably because of the additional weight entailed. Less obvious was an increase in length by 46ft. This additional space was used for another three boilers, which created a 29 per cent increase in power and resulted in an additional knot of speed. Armour protection was increased and was superior to all British battlecruisers. The placement of the waist turrets was far enough apart to give each turret an enhanced arc of fire on the opposite beam.

Seydlitz was laid down at the Blohm und Voss yard and completed in 1913. She participated in all major actions of the German battlecruiser fleet and survived extreme damage at Jutland. Scuttled in June 1919, she was raised and scrapped in 1928.

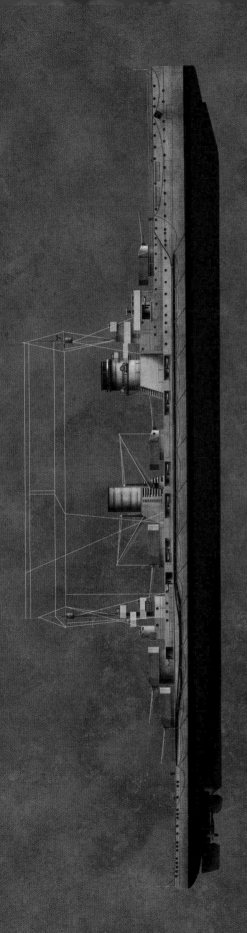

Seydlitz pictured before the war; note the arrangement of the inefficient waist turrets. The raised forecastle, making the ship unique among German battlecruisers, is evident. (Cody Images)

DERFFLINGER CLASS

The final German battlecruiser class to be completed comprised the three ships of the Derfflinger class. These were arguably the best battlecruisers to see action during the war and came closest to being fast battleships. This was the first German battlecruiser class to be mounted with a main battery of 12in guns. Only four twin turrets were fitted but these were moved into forward and aft positions with one of the turrets in a superfiring position. For the first time, no waist turrets were fitted. This gave the ships a balanced and aesthetically pleasing appearance. The lack of waist turrets allowed different and more compact arrangements of the boilers, reflected by the fact that the two stacks were positioned close together. Length was increased and beam

Derfflinger absorbed tremendous damage from heavy-calibre shells and still managed to return to port. A total of at least 21 shells struck the ship – ten 15in, one 13.5in and ten 12in. This is a view of the port side and shows one of the destroyed 5.9in guns and the damaged torpedo nets on the side of the hull. (IWM Q 20762)

actually slightly reduced, which resulted in a greater length-to-beam ratio and a similar speed to the preceding *Seydlitz* despite a slight reduction in power.

The three ships were not laid down until 1912, and thus only *Lützow* was ready for Dogger Bank in 1915. Both *Lützow* and *Derfflinger* took part in the action at Jutland, with *Lützow* being lost. She was the only German battlecruiser lost during the war. *Hindenburg* took 47 months to build and was not completed until after Jutland. She and *Derfflinger* were both surrendered after the war and scuttled in June 1919. *Derfflinger* was not raised until 1939 and not scrapped until 1956; *Hindenburg* was raised in 1930 and broken up in 1932.

Derfflinger firing her main battery. The class were the first German battlecruisers to be equipped with 12in main guns. (Cody Images)

Derfflinger class	
Ships in class:	*Derfflinger*, *Lützow*, *Hindenburg*
Displacement (normal):	26,500 tons
Dimensions:	Length 690ft; beam 95ft; draught 31ft 6in
Armament:	Eight 12in/50 guns; 12 5.9in guns; eight 3.5in guns; four 19.7in torpedo tubes
Protection:	Main belt 12in (maximum); deck 3.2in; turrets up to 10.75in (face), 8.75in (sides), 4.3in (top); conning tower 14in (maximum); barbettes 10.25in; torpedo bulkhead 2in. Total weight of armour: 9,840 tons
Machinery:	Four Parsons turbines driving four shafts; 18 (14 coal and four oil-fired) boilers creating 63,000shp (design); top speed 26.5kt
Range:	5,400nm at 14kt
Crew:	1,390 (1916)

SMS LÜTZOW

THE COMBATANTS

The crews of both navies' battlecruisers were well-trained and motivated, and possessed high morale. British crews had centuries of naval tradition behind them and the dashing battlecruisers epitomized the daring and fearlessness of the Royal Navy. They were certain that when they had the opportunity to meet their German counterparts then British victory would be assured. The Imperial German Navy, though still a new force dating back only to the unification of Germany, and much more recently seen as a rival to the mighty Royal Navy, was also confident. Its ships and technology were first rate and training on an individual ship basis was meticulous and prolonged. The new Imperial German Navy yearned to be let off the leash to show the British what they were capable of in an all-out contest. With both sides skilled and eager for battle, the question of the quality of personnel would not be the deciding factor in the impending clash between the battlecruisers. The battle would be a test of the two sides' tactics and technology.

TACTICS

BRITISH

Before the start of World War I, the Royal Navy had largely ignored the development and dissemination of tactics. Those tactics that were in place had been updated by Fisher. The standard tactical formation was the 'line ahead'. This was preferred for several reasons. It did not mask the guns from other ships in the formation and it was flexible. Perhaps most important of all, it had the virtue of simplicity, which reduced

OPPOSITE
Lützow was a member of the Derfflinger class, which represented the last German battlecruiser design and was the finest battlecruiser design to see action during the war. The ship can be recognized by its flush main deck with its pronounced sheer forward. The main battery of eight 12in guns can clearly be seen. Despite the ship's heavy armour, *Lützow* did not survive the heavy pounding it received at Jutland. *Lützow* was the only German battlecruiser lost during the war.

45

both the potential for confusion and the requirements for signalling. Another consideration was that unlike in an open formation, a line ahead reduced the problem of discerning friendly ships from enemy ships. Even in daylight, this could become a real problem when all the smoke from ships and their guns decreased visibility. Reduced visibility in the form of haze was also a factor in the North Sea, where the anticipated clash between battle fleets was expected to occur.

Much thought had been given to achieving superiority of fire. It was assumed that the battle would be fought between two forces steaming in parallel in line-ahead formations. The British, with numerical superiority, had devised and practised ways of concentrating the fire of several ships on a single target. Usually, with the shells of more than one ship falling around a target, this was difficult to do since the numerous splashes made correcting fire more challenging.

The battlecruiser was a useful tool to aid in the goal of achieving concentration of fire. The main role of the battlecruiser and its associated light cruisers was scouting for the battle fleet. It was crucial that the scouting forces provided adequate warning on the location, speed and course of the enemy fleet so that the friendly battle fleet could deploy out of their steaming formation of multiple columns into their line-ahead battle formation. The speed of the battlecruisers also offered the potential of their operating as a 'fast wing' of the battle fleet, which could be deployed to the van or the rear of the formation to achieve tactical superiority.

The use of radios made it possible for the British to envisage the use of battlecruisers at a greater distance from the battle fleet. The farther they operated from the main fleet, the more warning the fleet commander had to plan the movements of the battle fleet as he sought to bring the enemy battle fleet into action. As the war developed, the battlecruiser fleet became an independent entity and was even based separately from the battleships of the Grand Fleet. The speed of the battlecruisers made them more likely to engage the Germans and this became even more important after the Germans began a series of raids on the British coast. Even as British intelligence provided advance warning of German fleet operations, the British battleships and battlecruisers operated as separate elements. Usually, they co-ordinated their actions and planned a rendezvous at a specified location like in May 1916 at Jutland.

When Admiral Sir John Jellicoe (1859–1935) took command of the Grand Fleet at the start of the war, he stressed the need for the British to engage the Germans at long ranges, exploiting what he saw as the British advantage in gunnery, and to avoid all potential underwater threats. He believed that the Germans sought a close-in battle and that they would make up for their deficiency in capital ships with their fleet of heavily armed destroyers. By the time of the battle of Jutland in May 1916, Jellicoe had become even more conservative. By this time, it was obvious that the Germans were not seeking to engage the British except under the most tactically advantageous circumstances. Jellicoe was well aware of the lack of underwater protection on British capital ships since he was involved in their design before the war, and was determined not to risk the fleet in battle against underwater threats. The primary mission of his destroyers was defending against German torpedo-boat attack, not launching their own attack on the German battle fleet.

As conservative as Jellicoe was (and he had to be to preserve British naval superiority), Beatty went to the other extreme. As the dashing young commander of the hard-charging battlecruisers, his mission was to find, engage and destroy the enemy. Only when the German battle fleet was detected would he modify his basic tenet of closing with the enemy. In this particular case, he would retreat in the face of superior firepower and lead the Germans into the grasp of the overwhelming firepower of the Grand Fleet, where they would meet their final destruction.

GERMAN

German tactics were less mature than those of the Royal Navy. This is not surprising since the German High Seas Fleet had only been created in 1907. At the start of the war, the Germans believed (or perhaps more accurately wished) that the British would institute a close blockade of the German naval bases in the North Sea. This would allow the Germans several tactical advantages that could compensate for the larger size of the British battle fleet. In general, German fleet-sized operations were marked by poor planning, but the Germans were excellent at the individual or small-unit level.

The pre-war tactics of the High Seas Fleet called for the creation of several scouting groups, which would be deployed at the front and rear of the main battle fleet. This deployment would help the Germans to avoid the possibility of surprise from any direction. These scouting groups consisted of battlecruisers and light cruisers. The German fleet was not well balanced, and the scouting forces were inadequate both in numbers and in capability. Most of the light cruisers were too small and poorly armed to operate independently, and there were few battlecruisers available. The battlecruisers made up I. Aufklärungsgruppe (I Scouting Group), which would be deployed in the middle of the scouting force so that they could support the light cruisers. It was desired that the scouting forces be deployed some 25 miles ahead of the main battle fleet to prevent enemy scouts from sighting the German battleships too soon and to give the German battle fleet time to deploy in a fighting formation when the time came.

The role of the scouting groups led by the battlecruisers was critical. The entire German naval strategy depended on subjecting the superior British battle fleet to attrition over time until reaching a rough parity allowed a fleet engagement. The battlecruisers provided tactical warning and determined when and if the Germans would accept action.

Unlike the British, in a gunnery duel between capital ships, the Germans wanted to close as soon as possible to fight at the range of 6,600–8,800yd. This would allow the Germans to use their medium guns and torpedoes as well as their main batteries. The Germans intended to close to this range by zigzagging to decrease the effectiveness of British long-range fire. If the situation developed unfavourably, the Germans practised a manoeuvre called the 'battle turn away'. This called for every ship in the battle formation to conduct a simultaneous turn away from the enemy. Since it was conducted by individual ships and not as a column, this drastic and sudden course change presented a good chance of breaking contact with the enemy.

During the battle-fleet engagement, the German battlecruisers would lead a fast division that could attack the head of the British formation and engage enemy light forces threatening the German battle fleet. German battlecruisers also played an important role in protecting the German destroyers from attack (thus preserving them for a critical moment) and in supporting them when they attacked the British fleet.

VICE-ADMIRAL SIR DAVID BEATTY

Beatty led a charmed career and would forever be linked with the Royal Navy's battlecruisers. Born in 1871, he entered the training ship *Britannia* in 1884 and graduated without distinction. His early career indicated no great ability, and it appeared stalled until 1896 when he got an appointment as second-in-command of the gunboats assigned to assist in the campaign to advance up the Nile to recapture Khartoum. In this capacity, his leadership abilities were noticed and his gunboats played a key role in the successful campaign. His efforts earned him early promotion to commander and a Distinguished Service Order.

More excitement for Beatty came in 1900 when he was sent ashore to fight the Boxers in China. He was wounded, but returned to Britain a hero. In 1902, he returned to sea as the commanding officer in a succession of cruisers. In 1905, he was thought of highly enough by the Admiralty to be appointed as the Naval Advisor to the Army Council. He continued to punch all the right career tickets and returned to sea to command a battleship; by 1910, assisted by Fisher, he achieved the Nelsonian distinction of reaching flag rank at the tender age of 38.

After refusing to take the appointment as second-in-command of the Atlantic Fleet, Beatty was rescued from career wilderness by Churchill in 1912. Churchill, as First Lord of the Admiralty (the political head of the Royal Navy), took Beatty as his Naval Secretary and Beatty impressed his new boss. When it came time for Beatty to return to sea, Churchill secured the command of the 1st Battlecruiser Squadron for him.

As commander of the Grand Fleet's battlecruisers, Beatty assumed that the German battlecruisers had a mission similar to his. He was confident that in any action against his German counterparts, he would enjoy a numerical advantage. Beatty intended to press this advantage with his superior firepower to destroy the Germans. He intended to use his speed advantage to cut them off from the bases. Though mindful of the underwater vulnerability of his ships and the potential German threats in that regard, he did not let these factors interfere with his desire to engage and destroy the Germans. This basic approach was exemplified early in the war at the battle of the Heligoland Bight, in which his battlecruisers rushed to the scene of a clash between German and British light forces. The battle was the first British victory of the war and made the aggressive Beatty an instant national hero.

At Jutland, Beatty was not at his best. He seemed genuinely surprised his ships were so vulnerable and was clearly bested by his German counterpart. His handling of the battle was faulty in a number of areas. The numerical advantage he was counting on was squandered by his inability to bring the 5th Battle Squadron into action during the opening phase of the battle. When he spotted the German battlecruisers, he was not able to bring his longer-range guns into play and let the Germans open fire at the same time as he did. His constant course changes during the approach hindered the ability of his gunnery crews to determine target range. German gunnery was far superior to that of his battlecruisers' crews (as was that of Jellicoe's battleship crews). To some degree, this was Beatty's responsibility; although there were no practice gunnery facilities at Rosyth where the Battlecruiser Fleet was stationed, this was a problem about which Beatty had been previously advised, and he had taken no measures to correct the situation. Throughout the battle, command and control was an issue, primarily because of bad signalling. Again, Beatty must be seen as responsible, since the same problem was evident at Dogger Bank and he had done nothing about it. Finally, when he approached the Grand Fleet at the end of the 'run to the north', he failed in his primary duty to provide a clear and detailed report to Jellicoe on the position, course and speed of the German fleet.

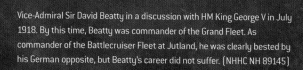

Vice-Admiral Sir David Beatty in a discussion with HM King George V in July 1918. By this time, Beatty was commander of the Grand Fleet. As commander of the Battlecruiser Fleet at Jutland, he was clearly bested by his German opposite, but Beatty's career did not suffer. (NHHC NH 89145)

KONTERADMIRAL FRANZ HIPPER

The commander of I Scouting Group, which consisted of the Imperial German Navy's battlecruisers during both battlecruiser clashes, was Franz Hipper (1863–1932). He was born south of Munich in 1863. He decided to join the new Imperial German Navy and entered the service in 1881. Hipper's early career led him to specialize as a torpedo officer. In command of a torpedo-boat squadron in 1902, he performed well and won promotion; later, he commanded I. Torpedo-Division and then SMS *Friedrich Carl*, an armoured cruiser. In 1907, the crew of *Friedrich Carl* won the award for the best gunnery ship in the fleet. By 1912, he was serving as deputy commander of the fleet scouting force and had achieved flag rank. A year later, Hipper assumed command of I Scouting Group.

As commander of the battlecruiser force, Hipper performed solidly in the November and December 1914 raids on the British coast. At Dogger Bank in January 1915, Hipper's force was the target of an elaborate trap set by the British, who had advance notice of the operation. Hipper made the British task easier by including the slow armoured cruiser *Blücher* in his force. Chased by Beatty, Hipper and his three battlecruisers only escaped when signalling errors led the British to focus on the unfortunate *Blücher*. The fact was that in this tactical defeat for the Germans, Hipper's ships had shot better than Beatty's and had more than held their own. Instead of being blamed for the loss of *Blücher*, Hipper received a decoration from the Kaiser.

After Dogger Bank, Hipper went on sick leave for five weeks during which time his boss, Vizeadmiral Reinhard Scheer (1863–1928), tried to get him retired. This ploy failed and Hipper returned to duty in May 1916. The clash at Jutland occurred just days later, and saw Hipper's battlecruisers sink three British battlecruisers. However, Hipper's flagship, the new *Lützow*, was sunk. Overall, Hipper performed well at Jutland. Though outnumbered, he had inflicted heavy losses on Beatty and delivered the British battlecruisers to potential destruction at the hands of Scheer's battleships. Despite a fearful pounding, Hipper was able to bring four of his five battlecruisers home. Hipper's ships were responsible for inflicting the heavy losses suffered by the British and it was on this basis that the Germans could declare with some justification that the battle was a great victory. For this role, Hipper received Germany's highest military honour, the *Pour le Mérite*, from the Kaiser on 5 June. He was also elevated to the Bavarian nobility and given the title *Ritter*.

Hipper upheld his reputation as an experienced sea dog during the war. He was an effective, though not flashy, battlecruiser commander. It is worth noting that of the four principal admirals engaged at Jutland, only Hipper emerged with his reputation clearly enhanced.

Franz Hipper was the commander of the German battlecruiser force at both Dogger Bank and Jutland. He performed solidly, but not spectacularly, at Jutland and when given the opportunity to engage the British battlecruisers on near-equal terms, he took advantage of it and sank two British ships in the opening stage of the battle. (Cody Images)

GUNNERY AND FIRE CONTROL

BRITISH

The key to victory in a clash between big-gun ships is the provision of accurate fire direction. With a target at long range, the ship's gunnery officer could not simply point his guns at the enemy and fire. To hit targets, the gun had to be fired in a trajectory, which meant that a period of time expired between the time it was fired and the time the shells landed. Thus, the fire-direction system had to predict the movement of the target during this time and feed this information to the guns. This required an accurate estimation of the enemy's range, course and speed, all of which were constantly changing.

The Royal Navy led the way in efforts to solve this complex problem. The solution was a device known as the Dreyer Table. Expressed simply, this produced a plot of the measured ranges to a target, which could be used to calculate a rate of change. The rate was fed into a clock and it provided a solution on a plot. This information was the basis for a fire-control solution.

Once the war began, the British discovered that figuring an accurate range was more important than figuring the rate of change. Range was gained by rangefinders, of which every capital ship had several. However, these were most often inaccurate, especially under poor-visibility conditions. This forced calculations to be gained by using an average of all rangefinders, and here the Dreyer Table proved very useful since it used the input from all the ship's rangefinders. As the war went on, more ships were equipped with a central director. These were mounted as high as possible on the ship to increase visual range, which meant the best place was the top of the foremast. The director controlled all the ship's guns and could more easily compensate for the roll of the ship. This system did have the effect of slowing down the rate of fire as opposed to each turret engaging targets on its own.

The pre-war British plans were to open fire at 15,000yd and then to decrease the range until maximum firing rates were achieved at 12,000–13,000yd. The British expected the effective range to be about 8,000–10,000yd.

GERMAN

Both sides envisaged that capital ships would only be lost as a result of the cumulative effect of shell-fire. The Germans were as surprised as the British when they quickly destroyed three British battlecruisers at Jutland. The Germans used half-salvos for capital-ship gunnery. This meant that one barrel per turret fired in a salvo and it had the effect of keeping the enemy constantly under fire.

The Germans did not adopt the British doctrine of using central directors. They did install fire-control tops as did British ships, but these were used as target designators. By Jutland, all of the battlecruisers had this director-pointer (*Richtungsweiser*) technology. These gave the correct training angle to the turrets, but in each turret the guns were laid and fired individually.

One advantage held by the Germans was the quality of their optics. Most battlecruisers employed 3m Zeiss rangefinders placed on each turret and in the fire-control tops. These were used for both the main and secondary batteries. These rangefinders were stereo unlike the coincidence ones used by the British. Rangefinder data was read in the fire-control tops. Unlike the British system, the data from the German rangefinders was not averaged, so if a rangefinder was providing inaccurate data, this was not immediately obvious. Overall, this system was much simpler than the British system and, in the hands of a well-trained gunnery officer, it was quicker. The negatives were that it was reliant on the quality of the gunnery personnel and could be totally ineffective if incorrect rangefinder data was used. The ship's fire was controlled by the gunnery officer in the armoured tower just above and abaft the conning tower.

COMBAT

THE BATTLE OF DOGGER BANK

At 1745hrs on 23 January, Hipper led his battlecruiser force out of port. Since *Von der Tann* was still under repair, this left the Germans with only three battlecruisers – *Seydlitz* (flagship), *Moltke* and *Derfflinger*. Hipper also decided to bring the armoured cruiser *Blücher* along to make up for his reduced numbers. The inclusion of *Blücher* turned out to be a key decision, since her top speed was 23kt, slower than even the oldest British battlecruisers. Accompanying the large cruisers were four light cruisers and 19 destroyers. If all went as planned, the force would proceed to the area of Dogger Bank, and return to base late on 24 January.

Since the British had intercepted and decoded Hipper's orders, there was little chance that things would go as the Germans planned. The Admiralty quickly put together a plan to bring overwhelming force against Hipper. To execute this planned interception, Beatty's battlecruisers left their base at Rosyth at 1800hrs, only minutes after Hipper's departure. Beatty sortied with his battlecruisers organized into two squadrons. Under his direct control Beatty had his flagship *Lion*, plus *Tiger* and *Princess Royal*. The 2nd Battlecruiser Squadron under Rear-Admiral Sir Archibald Moore (1862–1934) consisted of *New Zealand* and *Indomitable*. Accompanying the battlecruisers were the four light cruisers of the 1st Light Cruiser Squadron. An additional three light cruisers and 35 destroyers would join Beatty's force at a planned 0700hrs rendezvous on 24 January at a point north of Dogger Bank. Another force of armoured cruisers and a squadron of seven pre-dreadnoughts also departed Rosyth to be in a position to protect the east coast

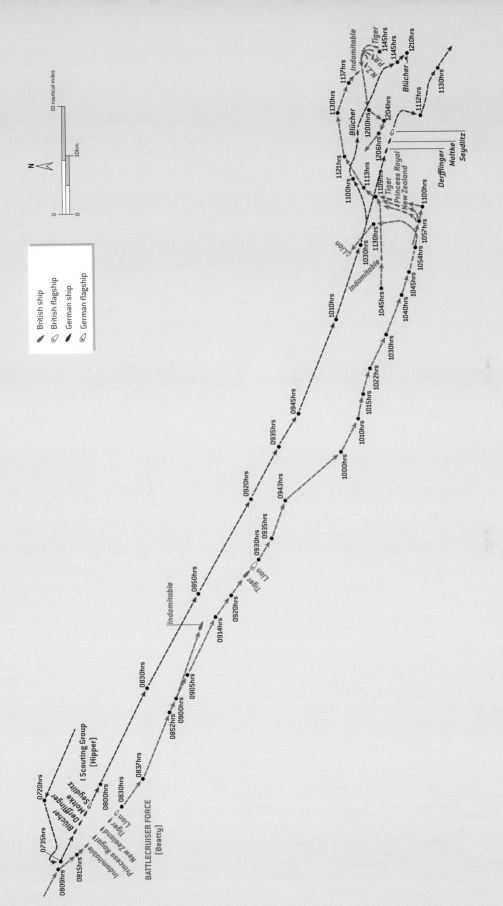

Dogger Bank, 24 January 1915.

Map labels:

Legend:
- British ship
- British flagship
- German ship
- German flagship

N

10 nautical miles
10 km

BATTLECRUISER FORCE (Beatty)

I Scouting Group (Hipper)

Blücher
Derfflinger
Moltke
Seydlitz

Indomitable
Princess Royal
New Zealand
Tiger
Lion

Times (British track):
0809hrs, 0815hrs, 0830hrs, 0800hrs, 0837hrs, 0852hrs, 0900hrs, 0905hrs, 0914hrs, 0920hrs, 0930hrs, 0935hrs, 0943hrs, 0945hrs, 0935hrs, 0920hrs, 0850hrs, 0830hrs, 1000hrs, 1010hrs, 1015hrs, 1022hrs, 1030hrs, 1040hrs, 1045hrs, 1045hrs, 1054hrs, 1057hrs, 1100hrs, 1100hrs, 1109hrs, 1113hrs, 1121hrs, 1100hrs, 1030hrs, 1130hrs, 1010hrs

Times (German track):
0720hrs, 0735hrs, 0800hrs, 0837hrs, 1130hrs, 1137hrs, 1145hrs, 1145hrs, 1200hrs, 1204hrs, 1206hrs, 1210hrs, 1112hrs, 1130hrs

Ship labels on map: Indomitable, Tiger, Lion, Blücher, N.Z., P.R., Tiger, Blücher, Princess Royal, New Zealand, Tiger, Derfflinger, Moltke, Seydlitz

Princess Royal, which fought at Heligoland Bight, Dogger Bank and Jutland. At Jutland, she took nine heavy-calibre hits and suffered 22 killed and 81 wounded. She accounted for five 13.5in hits on two different German battlecruisers. (Library of Congress)

and to block Hipper if he moved north. The Admiralty assessed that these forces were sufficient to the task since the Grand Fleet was not informed of the operation until early afternoon and could not depart until 2100hrs. This meant that when the battlecruiser clash occurred, the battle fleet was 140 miles distant.

Beatty had high hopes that the 24th would bring a major victory. The rendezvous proceeded flawlessly at the point where the Admiralty reckoned Beatty could intercept Hipper's force. Everything was set to spring the trap on the unsuspecting Germans, and even the North Sea weather was favourable with calm seas and perfect visibility.

The battle began with a clash of the light cruiser screens at about 0720hrs. Steering to the sound of gunfire, Beatty's battlecruisers soon gained visual contact on the German force and identified their German counterparts. Anxious to avoid his prey from escaping, Beatty made a course to the south-east at full speed to take advantage of the wind direction in order to keep his smoke clear of his ships and to eventually get between the Germans and their bases. Hipper's initial response was uncertain, since he thought that the initial reports indicated that only scattered light British forces were present. As additional reports were received of a large concentration of smoke to the north-west and south-west, followed by a report of large numbers of cruisers and destroyers, Hipper assessed that he was in a trap. However, since he had intelligence that British battleships were present (not the speedier battlecruisers), at 0735hrs he ordered a course to the south-east at 20kt. The British followed, and a chase developed. It was not until the British were clearly gaining on him that Hipper realized that his opponents were in fact battlecruisers.

By 0750hrs, the British were closing the distance and Beatty saw the Germans on his port bow at a distance of 14 miles. To gain more quickly, Beatty ordered an increase in speed to 27kt at 0834hrs, and followed this with an order for 28kt, and then at 0854hrs to 29kt. This was considerably faster than the 23kt that Hipper's force was making, but the greater speed divided the British battlecruisers into two groups. Unable to make more than about 26kt, *New Zealand* and *Indomitable* fell behind. At 0845hrs, *Lion* opened the battle when she fired at *Blücher* at a range of 20,000yd. At 0900hrs, *Tiger* joined the battle, followed by *Princess Royal*. All three British battlecruisers fired slowly and deliberately at this extreme range using two-gun salvos from their forward turrets. The last two of Beatty's battlecruisers were still out of range. The first hit on *Blücher* was recorded at 0909hrs by *Lion*. The speed of the German armoured cruiser was reduced and her two aft turrets knocked out. The British observed a large fire amidships.

At 0911hrs, the Germans opened up with their main guns against the pursuing British. Only their rear and starboard waist turrets could be brought to bear. Throughout the action, the Germans were hampered by their own smoke. The initial focus of German attentions was the leading British ship, primarily because she was the only one in clear view. *Lion* was at a range of 18,000yd, much more distant than the ranges at which the Germans expected to fight a gunnery duel.

Within minutes of the opening German salvos, *Lion* shifted her fire from *Blücher* to *Derfflinger*. At 0928hrs, *Lion* took the first of 16 hits she would suffer during the battle. The first hit was an 8in shell from *Blücher* that hit the battlecruiser's forward turret. The shell did not penetrate, but it did disable the crew and put the left gun in the turret out of action. *New Zealand* joined the fray at 0930hrs when she opened fire at *Blücher*.

Now sure he was facing battlecruisers, Hipper had increased speed to 23kt, which was the top speed of *Blücher*. At this speed, the British continued to gain, and the battle entered a new phase. At 0935hrs, with the range down to 17,500yd, Beatty ordered each of his battlecruisers to engage the opposing ship in the German column. His intention was to have *Lion* engage *Seydlitz*, *Tiger* engage *Moltke*, *Princess Royal* engage *Derfflinger* and *New Zealand* continue to fire on *Blücher*. *Tiger*'s commander, Captain Henry B. Pelly, thought that *Indomitable* was already firing on *Blücher* (she was actually still out of range), which would have meant his opposite was the lead German ship, *Seydlitz*. He decided to fire on the lead German ship, which left *Moltke* unmolested. Beatty ordered this for two reasons. Aside from its simplicity, this method of fire distribution had two key advantages. Firstly it was easier to spot the fall of shot and make corrections if only one ship was engaging a target, and it was also desirable to bring every enemy ship under fire so that they did not have an opportunity to fire and make corrections undisturbed.

The early minutes of the main phase of the battle went favourably for Beatty. At 0940hrs, *Lion* scored a devastating and potentially fatal hit on *Seydlitz*. A 13.5in shell penetrated the quarterdeck and hit the barbette of the German ship's rear turret. It did not penetrate the 9in of armour, but hot fragments from the armour entered the shell-handling room where they hit charges and created a large fire. The fire burst into the turret and down the barbette. Men escaping the fire opened the hatch connecting to the turret just forward, which allowed the fire to enter the adjacent handling room and go up into the turret. Both rear turrets were knocked out and their crews killed. The ship was in danger of blowing up if the aft magazines were penetrated by fire. This was prevented by the executive officer flooding both rear magazines.

The Germans shot well and soon scored against Beatty's flagship. At 1001hrs, a single shell from *Seydlitz* struck *Lion*. The hit pierced the belt armour, and water got into a switchboard space, short-circuiting two dynamos. *Lion* took a list to port. This was followed by another pair of critical hits by two shells from *Derfflinger* at 1018hrs. These led to saltwater contamination of the boiler freshwater. These hits were the key events of the battle, as they led to *Lion* being forced to leave the battle along with Beatty. By 1052hrs, *Lion* had been hit by 14 shells, demonstrating the ability of battlecruisers to take damage. *Lion* had 3,000 tons of water in her hull. Her port engine stopped and speed was reduced to 15kt.

OVERLEAF
The battle of Dogger Bank quickly turned into a stern chase with Beatty's battlecruisers pursuing the retreating Germans. This scene shows the situation at about 1030hrs, the moment when the two battlecruiser forces were roughly abeam of each other. The German line was led by *Seydlitz*, followed by *Moltke*, then *Derfflinger*, then the armoured cruiser *Blücher* (out of view). The German ships are all steaming at high speed, thus heavy smoke from their stacks is evident. All three German ships are firing on the British ships, which are to their starboard quarter.

Blücher capsizing during the battle of Dogger Bank. The vessel was unable to keep up with the rest of Hipper's formation and became the only major ship lost in the battle. Hipper's three battlecruisers were able to escape after command and control difficulties led the British force to concentrate on the wounded *Blücher*. (NHHC NH 43105)

As *Lion* fell out of column, Beatty was already losing control of the battle. At 1054hrs, after personally spotting a submarine periscope, Beatty ordered a turn to port. This had the effect of crossing the wake of the German force, which moved Beatty's from Hipper's beam to astern of the Germans. This allowed the Germans to gain distance and it confused the rest of Beatty's battlecruiser captains. The confusion was increased when Beatty tried to signal his ships to stay after the fleeing Germans and leave the crippled *Blücher* to *Indomitable*. Since radios were not considered reliable, the primary method of issuing commands was by signal flags. Without an exact signal to indicate his intention, Beatty's signals officer had to pick the nearest equivalent from the signals book. This was 'Attack the rear of the enemy', but since the signal for the last course change was also still in effect, the signal was read as 'Attack the rear of the enemy bearing north-east'. Since Beatty was stuck on the crippled *Lion*, Moore was now in charge and he took the order to mean that Beatty was giving up on the chase and he was to concentrate on *Blücher*, located to his north-east.

At 1109hrs, the three lead British battlecruisers shifted fire from Hipper's force to the crippled *Blücher*. *Indomitable* had finally caught up and had been ordered by Beatty to finish off *Blücher*, which was now turning to port as a result of damage to her steering. Hipper considered trying to save the wounded *Blücher*, but with four battlecruisers around her, she was doomed. According to the official German history of the battle, *Blücher* took a significant number of large shells, estimated at about 70, and was also hit by two torpedoes. Just after noon, the armoured cruiser capsized and then sank. Film of this, which included her crew scrambling over the overturned hull, has been used ever since to show the sinking of a large ship. *Blücher*'s brave fight to the end impressed even the British. The price was heavy; of the crew of 1,026 men, only 234 survived to be picked up by British ships.

Blücher's desperate fight entailed the escape of the rest of Hipper's force. By the time Beatty could leave his flagship by destroyer and embark in *Princess Royal*, it was 1227hrs and the Germans were already 12 miles away and only 80 miles from Heligoland Island. The chase was over.

Dogger Bank was undeniably a British victory, but Beatty and everybody else involved on the British side felt it to be a shallow one. The escape of three German battlecruisers was a bitter pill, but the British believed they had heavily damaged *Seydlitz* and *Derfflinger*. In comparison, the British price of victory was low. Though struck by 16 shells, *Lion* only had 11 men wounded. The damage did require her to be towed back to Rosyth by *Indomitable* and repairs took four months. *Tiger* was hit six times but damage was minor, with nine dead and eight wounded.

Blame for the missed opportunity was quickly attributed to signalling errors and the lack of insight and aggression shown by Moore. The confusion caused by the poor signals could have been negated by Moore if he had better understood his commander's intent and acted with a touch of Nelsonian aggression. He was quietly moved to another command in February. A problem noted even at the time was the poor performance of British gunnery. The installation of a central director mounted in the foremast was sped up and by Jutland all battlecruisers were so fitted.

From the German perspective, the operation was not well conceived from the start, and given the British advantage in intelligence, Hipper was lucky to extract the bulk of his force from destruction. The inclusion of *Blücher* in the operation was a critical misstep, but ironically that actually resulted in the escape of the bulk of Hipper's squadron. The material cost of the operation was not great since the loss of *Blücher* counted for little. The damage to *Seydlitz* was considerable, but she was ready for action on 1 April. Three hits on *Derfflinger* caused only minor damage. The personnel cost was steep. Aside from the crew of *Blücher*, another 159 were killed on *Seydlitz* with another 83 wounded. Overall, the Germans had fought well and German gunnery had proved superior. Aside from the hits made on *Blücher*, most of which came at short range, the British only scored six other hits. The Germans had scored 22 hits, all at medium to long ranges. Perhaps most importantly, the near-destruction of *Seydlitz* forced changes to charge-handling procedures.

THE BUILD-UP TO JUTLAND

For the next clash, Beatty's force was organized into three squadrons and given a new designation as the Battlecruiser Fleet. The fleet remained based in Rosyth with the Grand Fleet still at Scapa Flow. While Dogger Bank was fought by the British with a

OVERLEAF
This scene shows the Battlecruiser Fleet in the opening moments of the battle of Jutland. Beatty is leading his battlecruisers south to cut the Germans off from their base. Beginning at 1548hrs, the two battlecruiser forces began to exchange fire. Here, Beatty's force, consisting of *Lion, Princess Royal, Queen Mary, Tiger* (not in view) and *New Zealand* (not in view), is steaming at full speed. The smoke from the British ships is blowing to their starboard side, which would prove an impediment as the gun crews attempted to gain target solutions. *Princess Royal* and *Tiger* are in the process of firing a broadside. *Lion* and *Princess Royal* are already under fire.

The Indefatigable-class vessel *Australia* collided with sister ship *New Zealand* on 22 April 1916 and was not repaired in time for Jutland. She survived the war and was scuttled in 1924 to comply with Washington Naval Treaty restrictions. (Cody Images)

Indefatigable under way in coastal waters before the battle of Jutland. Early in the battle, she became the first capital ship to be destroyed by another capital ship during World War I when she was struck by shells from *Von der Tann*. Only two from her crew of 1,019 survived. (IWM SP 392)

slim numerical advantage, the return of several ships from other duties and from the yards gave Beatty a total of nine battlecruisers.

Dogger Bank resulted in the dismissal of Friedrich von Ingenohl, though Hipper remained in favour. Ingenohl was replaced by Vizeadmiral Hugo von Pohl (1855–1916), who turned out to be even more cautious than his predecessor. The battle also proved that the current German strategy of relying on mines and submarines to reduce the measure of superiority enjoyed by the Grand Fleet was not working. Since the Kaiser now forbade the High Seas Fleet's new commander to venture beyond a day's steaming from its bases, and the British were equally unwilling to come that close to the German coast with capital ships, the prospects for another clash between capital ships was zero.

The failure of German naval strategy in the North Sea forced them to seek alternatives. It was decided to institute a blockade of commercial traffic with submarines. This included the sinking of ships within a designated war zone without warning, a measure sure to inflame opinion in neutral countries (principally the United States). The Germans proclaimed the waters around Great Britain to be a war zone on 4 February 1915 and the campaign began on 28 February. From the beginning, there were incidents involving neutral ships. These were of sufficient gravity that the Germans were forced to rescind their campaign by September. This was replaced with a restricted submarine campaign targeted against Allied shipping only. On 20 April, the United States issued an ultimatum, which forced a return to the restrictive prize rules.

The failure of the submarine campaign brought the High Seas Fleet back into play. Pohl died of liver cancer in February 1916 and was replaced by Vizeadmiral Reinhard Scheer, who was much more aggressive. Scheer immediately took a number of measures to increase the pressure on the British, hoping this might lead to an encounter that would present favourable tactical circumstances to inflict heavy attrition. The boldest of these was another raid on a British coastal town. On 24 April, Hipper's force departed for Lowestoft, supported by the entire High Seas Fleet. *Seydlitz* hit a mine, leaving four battlecruisers to conduct the operation. The British were aware that a major operation was under way, but bad weather on the following day prevented an interception of the Germans.

The British response to the Lowestoft raid was to launch another of a series of seaplane raids on German Zeppelin bases located along the North Sea on 4 May. The Germans did send out the High Seas Fleet in response, but the Grand Fleet had already left because of fuel issues. The pace of operations in the North Sea now made it much more likely that a major clash would occur. For his next operation, Scheer intended to raid Sunderland, his force supported by Zeppelins acting as scouts and submarines tasked with attacking responding British forces. Ideally, Scheer hoped that Hipper's battlecruisers would draw out the British battlecruisers, which he expected to sortie after the bombardment of Sunderland and then be drawn into the assembled might of the High Seas Fleet. This plan was postponed until the end of May to allow the completion of repairs to *Seydlitz*, and then was later changed to an attack on British light units and shipping in the Skagerrak, off the Danish coast.

As was the case in all of Scheer's operations, the entire High Seas Fleet was employed. The battlecruisers departed at 0100hrs on 31 May and were followed by the remainder of the High Seas Fleet. As usual, the British were aware of the impending operation by virtue of Room 40's outstanding efforts, and had departed their bases even before the Germans. Beatty left at 2300hrs on 30 May and Jellicoe led out the Grand Fleet at 2230hrs.

The battlecruiser forces of both sides were in the van of the operation. Hipper had all five available battlecruisers and selected *Lützow* as his flagship. Accompanying them were five light cruisers and 30 destroyers. Behind him by some 50 miles was the rest of the High Seas Fleet with 16 battleships, six pre-dreadnoughts, six light cruisers and 31 destroyers. This albeit very impressive force was more than matched by the Grand Fleet. Beatty's Battlecruiser Fleet was now comprised of three battlecruiser squadrons. One of these, the 3rd, had just been sent to Scapa Flow for scheduled gunnery drills and was with the Grand Fleet when it departed. The other two squadrons included six battlecruisers. Replacing the missing 3rd Battlecruiser Squadron were the most powerful battleships in the Grand Fleet, the four Queen Elizabeth-class ships of the 5th Battle Squadron under Rear-Admiral Sir Hugh Evan-Thomas (1862–1928). Escorting Beatty's heavy ships were 14 light cruisers, 27 destroyers and a seaplane carrier. The Grand Fleet sortied with 24 battleships, three battlecruisers, eight armoured and 12 light cruisers, 51 destroyers and a minelayer.

THE BATTLE OF JUTLAND

THE OPENING PHASE

While the British were aware that the German battlecruisers were at sea, it was not yet clear that the battleships of the High Seas Fleet were also present. Due to this misunderstanding (caused by confusion of critical information from Room 40), the Grand Fleet was making an economical speed in order to save fuel. This meant that it was not in a position to support Beatty as quickly as it might have, had Jellicoe been aware that the entire High Seas Fleet was at sea. This would take on critical importance later on 31 May. Beatty was ordered to steam easterly and if contact was not made by 1400hrs on 31 May, then to head north to rendezvous with the remainder of the Grand Fleet. These actions placed the British battlecruisers on a virtual collision course with Hipper's force, which was proceeding north up the coast of the Jutland Peninsula to a position off the entrance of the Skagerrak.

Lützow firing a salvo from her 12in guns during the battle of Jutland. As Hipper's flagship, *Lützow* led the German battlecruiser column; this view was taken from the armoured conning tower of *Derfflinger*. (Cody Images)

Without making contact, Beatty's force began its planned turn to the north at 1415hrs. The Germans were very close, with only 16 miles separating the cruiser screens of the two sides and only about 45 miles between the battlecruisers themselves. Given the position and course of the two sides, contact was inevitable. This occurred at about 1400hrs when the Germans stopped a Danish steamer. British light cruisers spotted the same ship, and then the German ships nearby. At 1428hrs, the light cruiser forces began to exchange gunfire. Within minutes, Beatty turned his force to the south-east in order to cut off the German force from its base.

The 5th Battle Squadron missed the initial flag signal to change course, and failed to make the turn. This created a gap between Beatty's battlecruisers and the battleships of nearly 10 miles and meant that their powerful 15in guns were unavailable for the first 20 minutes of the battle.

By 1445hrs Hipper had turned his force to the west and increased speed to 23kt. The two battlecruiser forces continued to close. At 1522hrs, *Seydlitz* recognized the British battlecruisers at 16,000yd. At 1545, the British made out Hipper's five battlecruisers. The scene was set for the largest clash of battlecruisers in history. At this point, the weather was favourable for a long-range gunnery duel with minimal wind, calm seas, and good visibility. By 1535hrs, the British were headed south in pursuit of Hipper. With ten capital ships to Hipper's five, and a marked advantage in heavy guns and broadside, Beatty believed that British victory was a certainty.

THE 'RUN TO THE SOUTH'

Hipper changed course 180 degrees to draw the British to the battleships of the High Seas Fleet, which was still steaming north. This phase of the battle is commonly referred to as the 'run to the south'. At this point, Scheer's lead battleships were only some 60 miles to the south. The British position was not as favourable. The Grand Fleet was some 70 miles north of Beatty's flagship and was now steaming south at 20kt. On his own initiative, Rear-Admiral Sir Horace Hood (1870–1916) led his 3rd Battlecruiser Squadron to the south-east at 25kt and was only about 45 miles north of Beatty.

On board the opposing battlecruisers, all crews were at their battle stations and the gunnery personnel concentrated on finding a firing solution. The British had a

In this view from light cruiser *Birmingham* at about 1600hrs, the Battlecruiser Fleet can be seen in action with flagship *Lion* leading *Princess Royal*, *Queen Mary*, *Tiger*, *New Zealand* and *Indefatigable*. German shells are exploding around the British column. Hipper's ships are not in view as they are well beyond the British battle line. (IWM Q 20889)

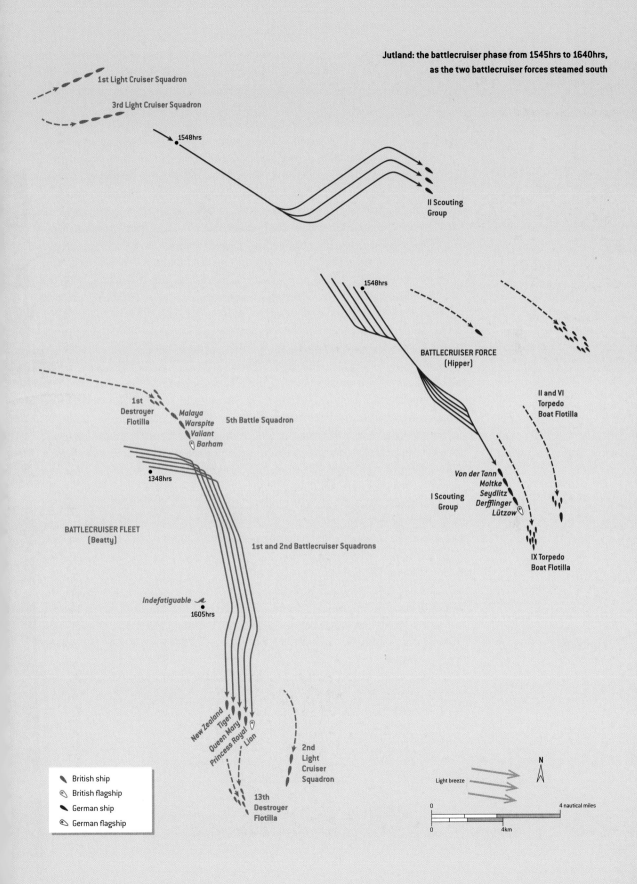

Jutland: the battlecruiser phase from 1545hrs to 1640hrs, as the two battlecruiser forces steamed south

1st Light Cruiser Squadron

3rd Light Cruiser Squadron

1548hrs

II Scouting Group

1548hrs

BATTLECRUISER FORCE (Hipper)

II and VI Torpedo Boat Flotilla

1st Destroyer Flotilla

Malaya
Warspite
Valiant
Barham

5th Battle Squadron

I Scouting Group

Von der Tann
Moltke
Seydlitz
Derfflinger
Lützow

IX Torpedo Boat Flotilla

BATTLECRUISER FLEET (Beatty)

1st and 2nd Battlecruiser Squadrons

1348hrs

Indefatiguable
1605hrs

New Zealand
Tiger
Queen Mary
Princess Royal
Lion

2nd Light Cruiser Squadron

13th Destroyer Flotilla

Light breeze

N

British ship
British flagship
German ship
German flagship

0   4 nautical miles

0   4km

tougher time finding the range since they were looking to the east into a grey sky and misty horizon. On the other hand, the Germans enjoyed the advantage of easily finding the dark-grey British ships against a westerly clear sky. The excellent German stereoscopic rangefinders were easily able to make out the British ships.

Perhaps because of this issue, despite having a range advantage the British held their fire. Hipper changed his course more to the south to close the range more quickly. At 1545hrs, Beatty responded with a change in course to the east-south-east and formed a column in preparation to open fire. The heavy guns of both sides opened up at 1548hrs. Since the 5th Battle Squadron was still trailing behind, the duel was almost even, with Hipper's five battlecruisers pitted against six British ships. Each of the German ships was ordered to fire on its opposite number in the British column. Thus, flagship *Lützow* targeted Beatty's flagship, *Lion*; *Derfflinger* engaged *Princess Royal*; *Seydlitz* engaged *Queen Mary*; *Moltke* fired on *Tiger*; and the last German ship, *Von der Tann*, fired on *Indefatigable*, which was the last British ship in the column. This left *New Zealand* untargeted. Beatty's fire-distribution plan was to use his slight numerical advantage to have his first two ships target *Lützow*, with each of the remaining four to take on its opposite number. However, *Queen Mary* did not receive the fire-distribution order, so she targeted *Seydlitz*. This left the second German ship, *Derfflinger*, unmolested for the first ten minutes. *Tiger* also failed to act according to Beatty's wishes and she fired on *Moltke* along with *New Zealand*. The net effect was that *Lützow* and *Moltke* were each fired on by two British battlecruisers, and *Von der Tann* fought a private duel with *Indefatigable* as did *Seydlitz* with *Queen Mary*.

Immediately, the Germans gained the advantage. The first British salvos landed a mile over their targets, but the Germans quickly found the range and scored within minutes. By 1551hrs, *Lion* and *Princess Royal* had been struck twice and *Tiger* four times. The forward turret on *Princess Royal* was knocked out and two turrets on *Tiger* were out of commission.

The first British ship to score was *Queen Mary*, which was generally regarded as the best gunnery ship in the Battlecruiser Fleet. Between 1555hrs and 1557hrs, *Queen Mary* scored hits at 12,900yd on *Seydlitz*, which knocked out one of her turrets. One of these hits was serious as it pierced the barbette armour of the after superfiring turret and caused a fire. Four charges were set on fire in the handling room and the fire spread up into the turret, killing most of the crew and disabling the turret. The fire also spread down into the magazine, but the measures introduced after Dogger Bank prevented a catastrophe. *Lion* also hit *Lützow* at 1600hrs on the bow, but no real damage resulted.

Lion seen on the horizon on fire after being struck on her midships turret. The shell that penetrated the turret caused a fire that spread to the working chamber 28 minutes later to explode eight powder charges. (IWM SP 1704)

In the opening minutes, the Germans had shot well, using four-gun salvos from each battlecruiser every 20 seconds. The excellent German rangefinders allowed them to find the range quickly. The British were forced to contend not only with unfavourable visibility as they looked to the east, but also with smoke being blown into their view by the west-north-westerly wind. This early German advantage was about to pay off in dramatic fashion.

At 1600hrs, *Lion*'s 'Q' turret was hit by *Lützow*. The shell penetrated the turret's side armour and exploded inside. The explosion wreaked havoc in the turret, killing almost everybody. Major F.J.W. Harvey, Royal Marines, was mortally wounded but managed to order the magazine doors below to be closed and the magazine flooded. Since burning charge bags were already falling into the handling room below, this undoubtedly saved the ship. Harvey was awarded a posthumous Victoria Cross. Six more hits followed against *Lion* in minutes. *Princess Royal* had another turret knocked out.

Lion under fire from German battlecruisers. Beatty's flagship narrowly avoided being destroyed by a shell from *Lützow* that penetrated the junction of the face and roof armour on the midships turret. Fortunately for the British, the magazine beneath the turret was flooded in time to avoid a calamity. (IWM SP 1712)

Much worse was to follow for the British. *Indefatigable* was hit by two or three 11in shells from *Von der Tann* at 1603hrs in the area of her after turret. Another two hits followed forward. None of these hits caused fire, but within 30 seconds, *Indefatigable* blew up. From her crew of 1,019, only two were rescued, by a German torpedo boat. *Von der Tann* had won her private duel in only 15 minutes and with the expenditure of 52 11in shells.

Soon, the range was down to between 11,500yd and 10,400yd. *Moltke* took the opportunity to fire four torpedoes at *Queen Mary*. All missed, but this served to throw the British column into further confusion as the consensus was that a U-boat was responsible. The situation for the British improved with the tardy arrival of the 5th Battle Squadron. By 1606hrs, each of the four British battleships turned its powerful main battery against the two rear ships of Hipper's force at a range of 19,000yd. The extreme range and the heavy smoke enveloping the target gave the British little prospect of success, but the Germans could not return fire. At 1609hrs, a 15in shell hit *Von der Tann* in her stern. At 1616hrs, another 15in shell hit *Moltke* but damage was limited to a single 5.9in-gun casemate.

While the British battleships intervened, Beatty changed course to open the range from Hipper. When the range reached almost 20,000yd, both battlecruiser forces ceased fire. Once it was evident Evan-Thomas had joined the fight, Beatty again changed course to re-engage. *Seydlitz* quickly scored additional hits on *Lion*, and by 1617hrs, *Derfflinger* and *Seydlitz* were firing on *Queen Mary*.

In the distance, *Indefatigable* can be seen after being struck by shells from *Von der Tann*. After the British ship fell out of formation, she was hit by another salvo, which resulted in her destruction with all but two of the crew of 1,019 being lost. (IWM Q 64302)

The range was down to 14,400yd when Beatty again changed course to open the distance. It was too late, though, for *Queen Mary*, which was under heavy fire from two German battlecruisers. At 1626hrs observers on other British battlecruisers saw her struck by three out of four shells from a German salvo and then two more from the next salvo. After a delay, there was a huge explosion amidships and then another in the forward part of the ship. The ship broke in two and quickly sank, except for the stern section, which lingered a few seconds more. A total of 1,266 men were lost. Only eight survived to be rescued by German and British ships. At this point Beatty turned to the commander of *Lion*, Captain Ernle Chatfield, and uttered his famous line: 'There seems to be something wrong with our bloody ships today.'

The first phase of the battle was about to come to an end and had gone about as well as the Germans could

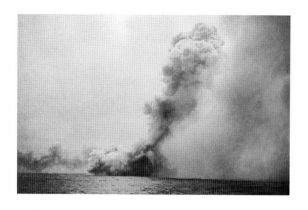

The huge smoke column marks the destruction of *Queen Mary* after being struck by a salvo from *Derfflinger*. The explosion cost 1,266 men their lives; there were only eight survivors, and two of these were picked up by German ships. (IWM SP 1708)

have hoped for, but with the weight of the battleships of the 5th Battle Squadron beginning to be felt, the odds were stacked against Hipper. Four of his five battlecruisers had been damaged, and *Von der Tann* had her combat power greatly reduced, with all but two guns placed out of action. Help was on the way in the form of Scheer's battle fleet, which was spotted by the battlecruisers as early as 1611hrs. The first indication that Beatty had of the arrival of the German battle fleet was given at 1638hrs by one of his light cruisers. Within minutes, the British battlecruisers spotted the columns of German battleships. The run to the south was over. Within five minutes Beatty's force was headed north to the safety of the Grand Fleet. With Jellicoe still some 60 miles to the north, the Germans were in a position to deal the British a crushing blow.

THE 'RUN TO THE NORTH'

Upon sighting the British, Scheer deployed his battleships in six columns and ordered full speed. The range was some 21,000yd, but the Germans opened fire on the fleeing British battlecruisers at 1638hrs. This was quickly stopped as the fire was ineffective at that range.

Hipper turned his ships to the north to be at the head of the High Seas Fleet. While they were executing their turn, the battlecruisers came under attack by British destroyers. One of their torpedoes hit *Seydlitz* at 1657hrs and blew a 40ft by 13ft hole in the forward part of the ship. In a testimony to the effective design of her underwater protection, *Seydlitz* was able to keep her place in the formation and still steam at full speed.

In a running battle, the German battlecruisers and the lead battleships continued to fire at Beatty's battlecruisers. Both *Lion* and *Tiger* were hit around 1700hrs, and Beatty was forced to steer to the north-west to open the range. By 1712hrs, the British battlecruisers had pulled out of range. This left only the 5th Battle Squadron in range, and it was on these four ships that the Germans now focused their attention. Despite firing for 30 minutes, the Germans were unable to score any critical hits. *Malaya*, the last ship in line, took several hits, but was able to maintain speed. Even while being showered with hits and near misses, the British battleships were able to maintain an effective fire against the pursuing Germans. Two of Scheer's battleships were hit by 15in shells, as were *Seydlitz*, *Lützow* and *Derfflinger*. Though not hit again during this time, *Von der Tann* had its last gun turret put out of action when it lost its recoil system. Even though his ship could no longer hit back, the ship's captain kept her in line so the British could not concentrate fire against the other ships in Hipper's squadron.

By this time, the visibility conditions had turned against the Germans. The sun was setting behind the British ships, which made it all but impossible for the Germans to observe the fall of shot. This was a factor when Beatty began to steer north-north-east to pass

In the distance, *Tiger* is steaming at high speed during the 'run to the north' during the second phase of the battle of Jutland. Only one 11in hit on *Tiger* was inflicted by the pursuing Germans during this part of the engagement. (IWM SP 2878)

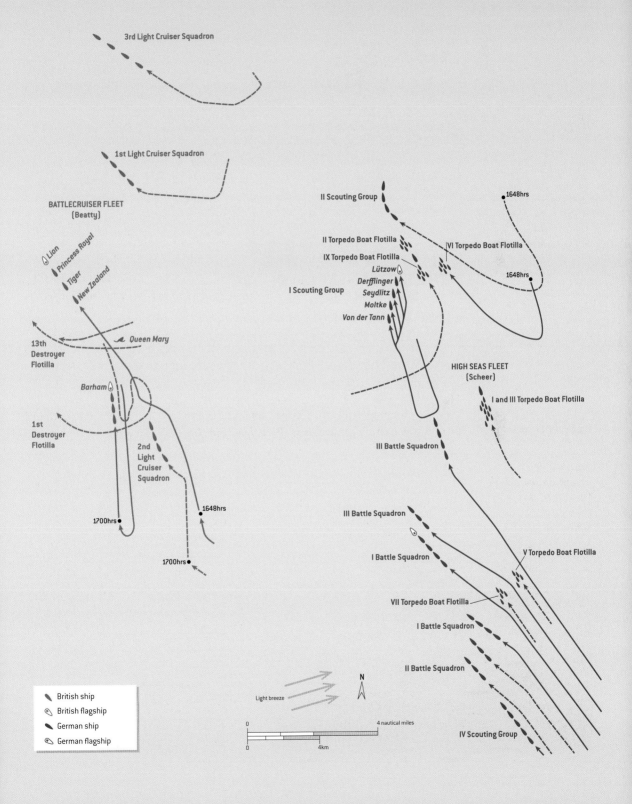

Jutland: the action from 1640hrs to 1745hrs, during the 'run to the north', when the High Seas Fleet engaged the British battlecruisers

3rd Light Cruiser Squadron

1st Light Cruiser Squadron

BATTLECRUISER FLEET
(Beatty)

Lion
Princess Royal
Tiger
New Zealand

13th
Destroyer
Flotilla

Queen Mary

Barham

1st
Destroyer
Flotilla

2nd
Light
Cruiser
Squadron

1700hrs

1648hrs

1700hrs

II Scouting Group

1648hrs

II Torpedo Boat Flotilla

VI Torpedo Boat Flotilla

IX Torpedo Boat Flotilla

Lützow

I Scouting Group

Derfflinger
Seydlitz
Moltke
Von der Tann

1648hrs

HIGH SEAS FLEET
(Scheer)

I and III Torpedo Boat Flotilla

III Battle Squadron

III Battle Squadron

I Battle Squadron

V Torpedo Boat Flotilla

VII Torpedo Boat Flotilla

I Battle Squadron

II Battle Squadron

IV Scouting Group

Light breeze

N

0   4 nautical miles

0   4km

British ship
British flagship
German ship
German flagship

Indomitable steaming in the wake of *Inflexible*, from which ship this photograph was taken during the third phase of the battle, which saw both main battle fleets engaged. *Indomitable* was the only Invincible-class ship to fight at both Dogger Bank and Jutland. (IWM Q 64308)

ahead of the German battlecruisers. Beatty's intent was to screen the Grand Fleet, which continued to pound down from the north. At 1740hrs, Beatty again opened fire. The 5th Battle Squadron divided its fire between Hipper's battlecruisers and the two lead battleships of Scheer's force. The Germans were virtually unable to respond under the existing visibility conditions. This marked the end of the run to the north. During this phase, the British gave a much better account of themselves, but all but one of the large-calibre hits scored by the British were attributable to the 5th Battle Squadron, not the battlecruisers.

THE BATTLE FLEETS COLLIDE

At 1800hrs, Beatty could see the battleships of the Grand Fleet. Soon, the combined British force was raining fire on Hipper's battlecruisers, to which the German vessels could make no effective reply. Hipper was forced to change course to the south-west to avoid the onslaught. This barrage placed a hit on *Derfflinger* and another hit on *Seydlitz*, allowing water to enter the former's bow section.

As the battle fleets prepared to clash, the agony of the British battlecruisers was not over. The three battlecruisers of the 3rd Battlecruiser Squadron were about to make their appearance. Hood had taken off at high speed on his own initiative when word was received that Beatty's force was engaged with the Germans. His intent to join forces with Beatty was thwarted by poor navigation and Hood ended up some 18 miles to the east of Beatty. At 1730hrs, *Invincible* heard gunfire to the south-west. The Germans were actually 14 miles away, but they were unseen through the mist. Ten minutes later, *Invincible* saw German light cruisers, and the British battlecruisers headed for them.

The appearance of the 3rd Battlecruiser Squadron on the unengaged side of the German formation was a great surprise to both Hipper and Scheer. At 1753hrs, *Invincible*, and then *Inflexible* and *Indomitable*, opened fire on a group of four German light cruisers. A 12in shell from *Invincible* hit the cruiser *Wiesbaden* at a range of 8,000yd, which destroyed her engine room. The ship came to a stop, and was later sunk. Another German light cruiser was hit, but remained in formation. Hood now came to a south-easterly course after seeing Beatty's approaching force with the Germans right behind.

In a heavily retouched but often seen photograph, this is the moment of *Invincible's* destruction following a 12in shell hit by *Derfflinger* on the British ship's amidships turret. It marked the third time during the battle that a British battlecruiser was destroyed by a powder explosion. (NHHC NH 354)

70

By 1805hrs, the Germans had turned around and a second race to the south was under way. Hood's battlecruisers had taken station in front of Beatty's flagship by 1822hrs. Hipper's battlecruisers came under fire from all three British battlecruiser squadrons. *Invincible* and *Inflexible* engaged *Lützow* at 9,600yd and *Indomitable* took on *Derfflinger*. Beatty's ships fired at the rear of the German line. This was a deadly combination. In eight minutes, *Invincible* fired some 50 rounds on *Lützow* and scored eight times. This was the best shooting of any ship during the battle. Two of the eight hits were below the thin armour belt in the bow, which created flooding. *Lützow* was forced to pull out of line and steam into the mist. This damage led to *Lützow*'s eventual loss.

However, *Invincible* did not have long to reflect on her success. *Lützow* and *Derfflinger* were both firing at her. After first falling short, the German shells soon bracketed *Invincible* and then inevitably began to score hits. The first hits were seen to hit *Invincible* astern, but with no effect. At 1834hrs, a salvo from *Derfflinger* hit amidships. One of the shells hit the face of *Invincible*'s 'Q' turret and burst inside. The top of the turret was blown over the side. This shell may have caused a flash down the turret barbette to the magazine below, or another shell from the same salvo may have hit the magazine. Whatever the case, the entire amidships section was engulfed in a huge fireball, which rose 400ft. The ship was destroyed instantly, but the two ends of the ship were left jutting above the surface of the water as the other ends rested on the shallow seabed. Only six crewmen survived, and four of these were from the director-control platform in the foremast. Hood was among the 1,020 men lost.

Beneath this massive plume of smoke is *Invincible* after she exploded. The photograph was taken from the next ship astern, *Inflexible*. (IWM SP 2469)

The remainder of the battle was dominated by the battle fleets. No further British battlecruisers were lost, but three armoured cruisers (each with a similar level of protection to the early battlecruisers) were sunk, two by magazine explosions that killed all or nearly all aboard. The German battlecruisers continued to take their place in the battle line and on one occasion were used to draw the fire of the Grand Fleet to enable Scheer's battleships to withdraw from a tactically disastrous situation. Of the five battlecruisers, all were damaged, but only *Lützow* was unable to return to base. The ship sank just before 0100hrs on 1 June. Before being abandoned, *Lützow*'s draft forward was 56ft and the ship's propellers were coming out of the water. All told, the battlecruiser took 24 large-calibre shell hits during the battle. *Seydlitz* took a nearly equal pounding with 22 hits, and was also down by the bow, but managed to return to port.

INDEFATIGABLE vs VON DER TANN

During the first phase of the battle of Jutland, HMS *Indefatigable* and SMS *Von der Tann* conducted a private gunnery duel. This **(1)** is the view from *Indefatigable* at about 1600hrs. The profile of *Von der Tann* is unmistakable since among the German battlecruisers it had a unique turret arrangement. Beyond the German ship, all that can be seen is a dull, grey sky and a misty horizon against which the British had difficulty reading ranges on the German ships.

As the private gunnery duel between *Von der Tann* and *Indefatigable* unfolded, disaster eventually befell the British. This **(2)** is the view of *Indefatigable* at 1603hrs. The profile of the British ship with its three widely placed stacks and two waist turrets clearly mark it as an Indefatigable-class ship. Beyond the fast-moving British battlecruiser was a clear sky and horizon, which greatly assisted *Von der Tann's* efforts to calculate a gunnery solution. The scene shows the effect of German gunfire. After *Indefatigable* was hit by shells from two separate salvos, and following an interval of some 30 seconds, the Germans observed huge explosions amidships and aft. When the smoke cleared, *Indefatigable* was gone and 1,017 men were dead.

1

2

STATISTICS AND ANALYSIS

In the biggest battlecruiser clash in history, the clear winners were the Germans. The Royal Navy lost three battlecruisers during the battle, and the Germans only one. However, it should be pointed out that *Lützow,* the single German ship scuttled, was the single most powerful ship lost by either side. British personnel losses on the three destroyed battlecruisers were astounding. A total of 3,309 men were killed, with only a total of 11 surviving from the three ships.

The first phase of the battle, the 'run to the south', gives the best opportunity to compare British and German battlecruisers. During this phase, lasting just over one hour, Hipper clearly defeated Beatty in spite of the fact that the Germans were heavily outnumbered in capital ships. The Germans destroyed two battlecruisers during this period while losing none themselves. An exacting analysis of the battle by British historian John Campbell confirms that German gunnery was more accurate. The five German battlecruisers scored 44 hits on the British – 42 on Beatty's battlecruisers and two on the 5th Battle Squadron. In return, the British scored 17 hits on Hipper's battlecruisers. However, of these, six were scored by the battleships of the 5th Battle Squadron and only 11 by the battlecruisers. Though the visibility during this period greatly favoured the Germans, the combination of better German rangefinders, superior protection and better armour-piercing shells proved deadly.

Within minutes of the magazine explosion, all that remained of *Invincible* were the bow and stern sections sticking out of the mud of the North Sea. These remained afloat for much of the remainder of the battle, marking the final resting place of 1,020 men. This photograph was taken from battleship HMS *Benbow*. (NHHC NH 349)

During the next phase of the battle, the so-called 'run to the north', the results were very different. The Germans scored 18 hits on five British capital ships (including battlecruisers *Lion* and *Tiger*). Of these 18, 11 were scored by three German battlecruisers. In return, the British placed 19 heavy shells on six German ships (including three battlecruisers). However, of this total, only a single hit was achieved by the battlecruisers, with the remainder going to the battleships of the 5th Battle Squadron.

In the next phase of the battle, which included the intervention of the 3rd Battlecruiser Squadron, both sides scored heavily. The German battlecruisers scored five hits, sufficient to destroy *Invincible*. In return, the British battlecruisers struck German capital ships with 14 heavy shells. Of these, ten struck *Lützow*, which led to her eventual loss.

Two British sailors looking through a shell hole in the forward turret roof of the battlecruiser *Tiger*. Overall she was hit 15 times by 11in shells during the battle of Jutland and lost 24 members of her crew killed and a further 46 wounded. (IWM SP 1597)

Battlecruiser gunnery at Jutland			
Unit	Shells fired	Hits	Hit percentage
1st and 2nd Battlecruiser Squadrons	1,469	21	1.43
3rd Battlecruiser Squadron	373	16	4.29
5th Battle Squadron	1,099	29	2.64
I Scouting Group	1,670	65	3.89

The statistics show that Beatty's battlecruisers shot poorly compared to the Germans and the battleships of the 5th Battle Squadron. The old battlecruisers of the 3rd Battlecruiser Squadron shot well, no doubt because they had completed gunnery training just days earlier. On the German side, the outstanding ship was *Lützow*, which placed 19 hits in 380 shots.

The effectiveness of British gunnery was reduced by the ineffectiveness of their shells. Of the 13 hits on heavy German armour, only one penetrated and burst inside. Seven failed even to pierce the armour. This tendency was even more pronounced on lighter armour between 6in and 9in.

Damage suffered by British battlecruisers at Jutland		
Ship	Number of heavy-calibre hits	Result
Indefatigable	5 (estimated)	Blew up
Invincible	5 (estimated)	Blew up
Lion	13	Heavy damage; repaired by 13 September
New Zealand	1	No repairs necessary
Princess Royal	9	Moderate damage; repaired by 10 July
Queen Mary	7 (estimated)	Blew up
Tiger	15	Moderate damage; repaired by 1 July

Battleship *Malaya* was part of the 5th Battle Squadron, which was attached to Beatty's Battlecruiser Fleet during Jutland. The heavily armoured ship was struck by seven 12in guns but suffered relatively light damage. The four ships of the 5th Battle Squadron all survived the battle and exhibited superior gunnery than had Beatty's battlecruisers. (NHHC NH 1085)

Damage suffered by German battlecruisers at Jutland		
Ship	Number of heavy-calibre hits	Result
Derfflinger	21	Heavy damage; repaired by 15 October
Lützow	24	Sunk by progressive flooding
Moltke	5	Moderate damage; repaired by 30 July
Seydlitz	22	Heavy damage; repaired by 16 September
Von der Tann	4	Moderate damage; repaired by 2 August

For the British ships that blew up, each loss could be attributed to poor protection. German shells penetrated the turret armour of *Invincible* and *Queen Mary*, as well as the horizontal armour of *Indefatigable*. Once they were penetrated in vital areas, the characteristics of the British powder and dangerous handling procedures made the ships very vulnerable, with the tragic results already described.

It needs to be pointed out that the same powder-charge problem and handling faults were present on all British capital ships. Nevertheless, only three battlecruisers exploded. This can be explained by the fact that the great majority of the Grand Fleet's battleships came under comparatively light fire at Jutland and none were hit in a turret. However, this cannot be said of the four battleships of the 5th Battle Squadron, which operated as part of Beatty's force for most of the battle and came under heavy fire. These ships were also the most heavily armoured battleships in the Grand Fleet, each having a main belt of 13in, barbette armour up to 10in and a maximum of 13in of protection on the turret faces. During the battle, *Malaya* was hit seven times by large-calibre shells, including once on the top of one of the rear turrets, but it was not penetrated. *Warspite* was struck 13 times, but not in any vital areas. *Barham* was hit six times, but again not in any critical areas. *Valiant* suffered only splinter damage. Through a combination of good fortune and good protection, these ships all survived. Compare this to the nine British battlecruisers committed of which three were destroyed.

Damage to *Derfflinger* caused by British heavy shells at Jutland. This view shows where shells have penetrated the deck, but not the heavily armoured barbette. A total of 157 men were killed aboard the ship and another 26 were wounded. (IWM Q 20765)

CONCLUSION

The question remains – was the battlecruiser effective? To answer this, the missions of the battlecruiser need to be kept in mind. These can be boiled down to protecting trade and acting as the main scouts for the battle fleet. In reality, these missions could have been carried out by an armoured cruiser with a standard 9.2in-gun armament. Fisher's demand for an all-big-gun ship with high speed was flawed from the start, since once assigned to the battle fleet as a scout, it would inevitably be used as any other capital ship. Once employed in such a manner, its lighter scale of protection was bound to jeopardize its survival. It also must be pointed out that battlecruisers were much more expensive to build than battleships since they were larger and had increased demands for machinery.

Seydlitz steaming to Scapa Flow in November 1918. The survival of the veteran battlecruiser at the battle of Jutland during the breakthrough of the High Seas Fleet to its bases during the early hours of 1 June was due to the fact that although no fewer than four British dreadnoughts spotted and identified *Seydlitz*, none of the British ships displayed the initiative required to engage the helpless German ship. (Cody Images)

The early British battlecruisers took Fisher's speed-is-armour dictum to extremes. Clearly the first two classes of Royal Navy battlecruisers were flawed ships, with protection no better than an armoured cruiser, speed inadequate to keep up with later battlecruisers, a broadside restricted to six guns, and an inadequate secondary battery. Later British battlecruisers exhibited increased firepower, speed and protection, but were never well-balanced ships.

However, it must be admitted that an examination of the ships themselves may miss the point of why they proved so vulnerable. The explanation for the destruction of the three battlecruisers at Jutland can be found not solely in the ships but in the magazine-handling procedures and the characteristics of British powder. This handling vulnerability was created by the British in an attempt to address an assessed weakness in their rate of fire. The result was a powder trail from the turret back to the magazine. Thus, when a turret was penetrated the ship could be lost. The catastrophic loss of the three ships at Jutland has given the battlecruiser a reputation for vulnerability. The lack of protection meant the ships' other shortcomings were fully exposed.

German design philosophy created battlecruisers that eventually merged into fast battleships. The result was ships that were as heavily armoured as many British battleships. Fortunately for the Germans, their designs were not tested by faulty explosive powder. Had the characteristics of German powder been more like those of British powder, *Seydlitz* would have been lost at Dogger Bank, and at Jutland it is probable that *Seydlitz* and *Derfflinger* would have both been lost. However, since the German battlecruisers each possessed a balance of protection, speed and firepower, they were undisputedly better fighting ships than their British counterparts.

Ultimately, the battlecruiser was a design dead-end, as the efficiency of machinery was increased while its size was reduced, making construction of fast battleships the norm. When World War II came around, the only battlecruisers being operated by the world's navies were hold-overs from World War I. The short and controversial life of the battlecruiser was over.

Hindenburg was the last German battlecruiser to be completed, but this came too late to allow the ship to see action at Jutland. She was essentially a repeat of the two earlier vessels of the Derfflinger class with minor improvements. This view shows the main battery arrangement of the most powerful battlecruiser class of World War I. A tripod foremast is evident in this view, but the other two ships in the class retained their pole masts in the Jutland battle. (Cody Images)

BIBLIOGRAPHY

Breyer, Siegfried, *Battleships and Battle Cruisers 1905–1970*, Doubleday and
    Company, Inc., Garden City, New York, 1973
Campbell, John, *Jutland: An Analysis of the Fighting*, The Lyons Press, New York,
    New York, n.d.
Campbell, John, *Battle Cruisers*, Conway Maritime Press, London, 1978
Corbett, Julian, *Naval Operations, Vol. II*, The Naval and Military Press, Uckfield,
    n.d.
Corbett, Julian, *Naval Operations, Vol. III*, The Naval and Military Press, Uckfield,
    n.d.
Friedman, Norman, *Naval Weapons of World War One*, Seaforth Publishing, Barnsley,
    2011
Goldrick, James, *The King's Ships Were at Sea*, Naval Institute Press, Annapolis,
    Maryland, 1984
Gordon, Andrew, *The Rules of the Game*, Naval Institute Press, Annapolis,
    Maryland, 2000
Greger, René, *Battleships of the World*, Naval Institute Press, Annapolis, Maryland,
    1997
Halpern, Paul, *A Naval History of World War I*, Naval Institute Press, Annapolis,
    Maryland, 1994
Hase, Georg von, *Kiel and Jutland*, Leonaur, 2011
Ireland, Bernard, *Jane's Battleships of the 20th Century*, HarperCollins Publishers,
    New York, New York, 1996
Marder, Arthur, *From the Dreadnought to Scapa Flow, Volume II: The War Years: To
    the Eve of Jutland*, Oxford University Press, New York, New York, 1965

Marder, Arthur, *From the Dreadnought to Scapa Flow, Volume III: Jutland and After*, Oxford University Press, New York, New York, 1966

Osborne, Eric, *The Battle of Heligoland Bight*, Indiana University Press, Bloomington, Indiana, 2006

Preston, Antony, *Battleships of World War I*, Stackpole Books, Harrisburg, Pennsylvania, 1972

Roberts, John, *Battlecruisers*, Naval Institute Press, Annapolis, Maryland, 1997

Roskill, Stephen, *Admiral of the Fleet Earl Beatty: The Last Naval Hero: An Intimate Biography*, Atheneum, New York, New York, 1981

Scheer, Reinhard, *Germany's High Seas Fleet*, The Battery Press, Nashville, Tennessee, 2002

Steel, Nigel & Hart, Peter, *Jutland 1916: Death in the Grey Wastes*, Cassell, London, 2003

Stille, Mark, *British Dreadnought vs German Dreadnought: Jutland 1916*, Osprey, Oxford, 2010

Tarrant, V.E., *Jutland: The German Perspective: A New View of the Great Battle*, 31 May 1916, Naval Institute Press, Annapolis, Maryland, 1995

Tarrant, V.E., *Battlecruiser Invincible: The History of the First Battlecruiser, 1909–16*, Naval Institute Press, Annapolis, Maryland, 1986

Young, Filson, *With the Battle Cruisers*, Naval Institute Press, Annapolis, Maryland, 1988

INDEX

References in **bold** are to illustrations